# EYDIE MAE'S NATURAL RECIPES

## FOR THE LIVEFOODS GOURMET

## EYDIE MAE HUNSBERGER
## And CHRIS LOEFFLER

## AVERY PUBLISHING GROUP INC.
### Wayne, New Jersey

Other Book By Eydie Mae Hunsberger
and Chris Loeffler
*How I Conquered Cancer Naturally*

Cover and Chapter Drawings by Boots Loeffler

Library of Congress Catalog Card Number 78-61660
ISBN 0-89529-229-7

# CONTENTS

# DEDICATION

We dedicate this book to the many friends who asked for it. We express our thanks to our many friends who have contributed recipes and suggestions for the book, with special thanks to Arn Hunsberger, our squire, for his constant encouragement, guidance and help.

Eydie Mae and Chris

"Whether therefore ye eat, or drink, or whatsoever
ye do, do all to the glory of God."
I Corinthians 10:31

# FOREWORD

Dr. Stanley S. Bass, N.D., D.C., Ph.C. says: "The closer the food comes to the natural state in which it occurs, or the closer we come to its raw, unfired form, the higher its quality is. In this condition, all the enzymes are found intact. The amino acids are in their finest form. The minerals, vitamins, trace elements, carbohydrates and life force are present. This life force, in turn, is capable of reproducing tissue which is full of life and longer lasting in structure."

Man is the only creature who tries to improve upon nature by cooking his food. Giving up cooked foods and living on raw, live foods has made many people feel well for the first time in their lives. Others who have been sick to begin with, switching to a raw, live food diet, have regained their health and feel better than they ever felt before.

The contents of this book is for the open-minded person, one who is ready for new suggestions and improvements . . . and a new way of living.

Raw foods can be fun as well as nourishing and "good for you", beautiful to the eye as well as practical, saving of energy as well as easy to prepare.

Everywhere Eydie Mae travels, aspirants to the "Living foods" diet ask her for new ideas for preparing the raw foods. Eydie Mae and Chris have combined their imaginations, their practical minds, their inquisitiveness, and their delight in eating out to bring you, "Eydie Mae's Natural Recipes," for the live food qourmet.

Chris Loeffler

# ARN'S TWO BITS

Eydie Mae and Chris have spent many hours selecting and sorting the recipes for this book so that everyone's tastes and diets were considered and yet so no one would be confused as to which recipes Eydie Mae would actually use at this time.

Perhaps a little explanation would be in order to clarify this question.

When Eydie Mae first started using live foods she was on what we term a therapeutic diet or Phase I. This was very strict and used no cooked foods at all.

After about three years on the therapeutic diet, she felt her health had improved to the point where she could expand her diet to include certain cooked foods which she has termed Phase II or a maintenance diet.

I would like to point out however that while attempting to regain her health she absolutely limited herself to the therapeutic or Phase I diet. From our study and Eydie Mae's experience, we have come to the realization that it is unwise to cheat where cancer or any of the major debilitating diseases are concerned because these diseases are unforgiving of even the smallest infractions of the rules of the Phase I diet.

To make it easier for you, the reader, little picture symbols have been placed beside each recipe indicating the phase applicable to that recipe:

Phase I  -   This phase termed "therapeutic" includes the recipes used by Eydie Mae during her recovery. These foods consist basically of uncooked fruits and vegetables plus sprouts and seeds. (See page 10 - Eydie has the last word.)

Phase II - This phase termed "maintenance" includes the recipes now used by Eydie Mae. These are foods in Phase I plus a few cooked foods such as brown rice, pinto beans, and baked yams, however she maintains 90% uncooked foods.

Phase III - This phase termed "the family" includes recipes to be enjoyed by family and friends who have not yet elected to try for the super health Eydie Mae and I feel we have derived from Phase I or II. These recipes are more nearly what they have been accustomed to and make great transition recipes for those whose health is good and are interested in experimenting to perhaps improve their health even more while enjoying a great eating experience.

The phases are progressive so that anyone enjoying Phase II may also utilize Phase I recipes and those experiencing Phase III may utilize both Phase I and Phase II recipes as well.

I was not ill when Eydie Mae was fighting for her life, however, I decided to eat just as she did due to my intense curiosity and the fact that it was just plain easier to handle the kitchen with a common menu. My adventure proved to be beneficial to my already good health and I learned to desire live foods over the way we had been eating, which was just the average American diet.

When I look back now it gives me cause to ponder what might have happened to both of us had we continued our sugar, salt and fried grease way of eating. I can assure you I have no desire to return to our previous body destroying, slow death diet and habits, which is the way we have come to look at our former way of eating.

Restricting my diet to the Phase II recipes the same as Eydie Mae, I experience good energy, good health and avoid all the little ills such as headaches, stomach aches and colds which I see our friends continually fighting.

Seldom a week goes by but one or the other of us, while enjoying a delicious meal, will comment that we feel that we are so fortunate to have discovered the best tasting food in the world! It took an adjustment period of from six months to a year before our tastes fully changed over to prefer the live foods. It is marvelous how the taste buds become more sensitive and the delicate differences in the many varieties of say peaches become very pronounced. Before, I thought peaches were peaches and they all tasted the same. Today we appreciate the delicate differences in the varieties and they appear to us to be as different and exciting in taste as day and night. Each year we look forward to the seasons as the many varieties of fruits and vegetables appear and disappear, and we can again enjoy the delicious and varied taste thrills we so crave.

We had some concern when we first started eating this way, that we would not be getting all of the vitamins, minerals and proteins that our systems required. Well meaning professionals and friends gave us warnings of impending pernicious anemia if our diet was not supplemented with animal products and store bought vitamins.

I would like to report that when Eydie Mae had her last blood analysis, the nurse brought out the report and exclaimed, "Wow! That's the blood test of an eighteen year old girl in perfect condition!" The total protein figure read seven which is considered perfect. This is the item most people are concerned about when contemplating an all live food diet. Eydie Mae's protein was derived in a certain degree from all of the foods she eats, but the largest contributors were avocados, sunflower and sesame seeds and sprouts.

I have given some thought on how to express my satisfaction with the live foods which would convey to you the gourmet pleasures and sensitive taste thrills which can be experienced by continued adherence to this way of dining. It's perhaps comparable to trying to verbally describe the various colors to a blind person who has never had sight so I will not attempt to do the impossible but will simply suggest that there are great new pleasures awaiting you on your adventure in live food gourmet eating. I sincerely hope that you find them as exciting and as satisfying as Eydie Mae, Chris and I have on our adventure.

Arn

(P.S. from Eydie)

## EYDIE HAS THE LAST WORD

In order to clarify the recipes in the three different phases even further, please note:
- If you omit oils, mayonnaise and nuts from any one of the recipes, they may be used for Phase I, II, or III.
- If mayonnaise is substituted for the seed sauces they become a Phase III only.
- Lemon juice may be substituted for mayonnaise or the seed sauces in any phase.

Eydie Mae

# RESTAURANTS

# HOW DO I EAT OUT?

**CHAPTER I.**

# CHAPTER I.

# HOW DO I EAT OUT?

## DID YOU KNOW THERE IS A
## HEALTH FOOD RESTAURANT CIRCUIT?

Southern California is alive with progressive, intelligent, adventuresome people looking for a better way of living. This same spirit is popping up all over the country. One of the ways they have discovered is eating healthier.

Ten years ago you had to experiment in your own kitchen and pretty much be considered a "health food nut".

No more.

The fastest growing restaurants today are the health food restaurants and people are coming out of the walls to eat in them and learn of them.

Impossible to tell you of them all, but we visited, ate in, and want to tell you of our impressions of just a few.

Have you been looking for a new adventure? Are you tired of trying to decide what to order of the conventional fare? Try ferreting out the Health Food Circuit. Then try adopting some of their glamor and refreshing ideas for yourself and your family.

## THE SOURCE RESTAURANT - 8301 Sunset Blvd. Los Angeles, CA.

All kinds of dining are found in one spot at the "Source."

You may choose dining outdoors on the patio in the front or the rear. Awning'd umbrella tables with wrought iron chairs invite you. There is even a breakfast bar.

Or you may prefer one of the two dining rooms inside on the first floor where a mirrored wall gives you the feeling of spaciousness and a maroon velvet draped picture window plus the fireplace filled with greens lends an air of class.

Upstairs, you'll find the informality of low tables with cushions on the floor and a guitar entertaining waiter.

Eight years in business, The Source was started by Jim Baker as a raw vegetable restaurant. After he formed a religious group, the brotherhood of the Source, and moved to Hawaii, the restaurant was sold to a corporation. The menu was enlarged at this time.

Ninety percent of the items on their menu are prepared to order. They juice all juices to order, and make their own ice cream.

## THE SOURCE RESTAURANT recommends their:

### "AWARE" Salad

| | |
|---|---|
| Wooden salad bowl | Tomato wedges |
| Lettuce | Avocado wedges |
| Bean sprouts | Cucumber slices |
| Pignolias (pine nuts) | Herb dressing |

Line your wooden salad bowl with lettuce. Pile the center high with sprouts and pignolias. Spotlight with red ripe tomato wedges interspersed with avocado wedges and cucumber slices.

Serve with herb dressing.

## *ENCINITAS NATURAL FOODS* - 120 1st St., Encinitas, CA

A cafe to pause and get refreshed, as well as a store in which to shop.

"Well, Hey, we're the best in the area — no kidding!", exclaimed one young man as he was unloading papayas and bananas from Mexico.

Later, the bright young man who manages the Encinitas Natural Foods, Tod Lee, chatted with us for awhile and shared some interesting insights about the present owner:

"He looks upon his store as a place of personal service. The store enables him to give young people in the area an opportunity for work.

"Not interested in shaking down the public, he has done a lot of improving, expanding, and re-investing of funds. After 2 years of ownership, the store is just starting to make a profit, and he is sharing the profits."

Several small high backed natural wood booths enable his customers to pause for awhile to refresh themselves with natural health foods such as tostadas, guacamole salad and drinks, although one would not regard the store as a full scale restaurant.

Tapestries decorate the walls while shoppers can buy groceries, food supplements, and a large selection of bottled juices, as well as thumb through 2 racks of shirts and tops for sale.

Customer service is good and store hours to accomodate the public are from 10:00 A.M. to 9:00 P.M.

As Tod Lee learned more about natural foods, he decided to try vegetarianism. Although he got sick going through the cleansing period (not unusual), he soon felt so much better that he has continued. He is experimenting with foot reflexology. His present goal is to become a naturopathic doctor.

The store is cheerful and unusual, a welcome stop along the way.

From the *ENCINITAS NATURAL FOOD STORE* (not on their menu, but a week-end special).

 **RAW VEGETABLE LOAF**

Grate lots of various vegetables such as:

| | |
|---|---|
| **Carrots** | **Cauliflower** |
| **Broccoli** | **Cucumber** |
| **Zucchini** | **Jicama** |
| **Yellow squash** | **Small amount of fresh onion** |

In a bowl combine brazil nut butter (made fresh) with a little tahini. Stir in tamari to taste. Mix with grated vegetables.

Press mixture into small individual loaf pans, turn out onto a plate lined with alfalfa sprouts and decorate with more raw vegetables.

 **TROPICAL CREME SMOOTHIE**

| | |
|---|---|
| ¼ **avocado** | **1 banana** |
| ½ **c. papaya** | **Honey** |
| ½ **c. coconut juice** | |

Blend until smooth in your blender.

*THE SHEPHERD* - 1126 S. Highway 101, Encinitas, CA.

Five years old as of January 22, 1978, the quaint charm of The Shepherd you have to behold to properly appreciate its beautiful secluded booths, grandmother clock and hanging plants in a natural wood background.

Another plus that they have going for them is their lovely outdoor patio in the rear, midst the growing gardens and more hanging plants, set with inviting tables and chairs to handle more customers.

Perry Rutledge, their manager, shared with us his belief that vegetarianism is not a fad — "it's a way of life."

After receiving training in catering and handling of food in other successful Natural Food Restaurants, they were inspired to serve the public in a restaurant of their own. Their success is undoubtedly commensurate with their desire to serve.

Classical guitar music is an added treat in the evenings.

Perry said, "The public has been good to us, even through the lean winters."

Perry Rutledge recommends *"AVOCADO BRAVO"* from "The Shepherd"

 **AVOCADO BRAVO**

| | |
|---|---|
| 1 lg. ripe avocado for each person | Chopped ortega chili |
| Cooked pinto beans or | Chopped raw tomato |
|   Cooked brown rice | Shredded jack cheese or cheddar |
| Chopped raw onion | Sprouts - optional |

Skin and pit the avocado. Fill each half with warm pinto beans or warm brown rice. Top with chopped onion, tomato, ortega chili, shredded jack or cheddar cheese (for Chris), (without cheese for Eydie Mae). Add sprouts if desired.

## THE MAGIC APPLE INN - 3522 W. Olive, Burbank, CA.

"What foods would keep the body clean and at the same time would fit into the category of good 'survival' foods?"

While answering these questions to his own satisfaction, Fred Koehler became a vegetarian six years ago. He also got involved in a Food Co-op, then became a cook for one of the better Natural Food Restaurants.

Today, he is one of the three owners of the Magic Apple Inn, all who find the restaurant business thoroughly enjoyable.

Celebrating 5 years in business during February 1978, Fred said, "The Magic Apple, naively and idealistically, started out to be a vegetarian restaurant."

They quickly found out they had to compromise — not on quality — but economics made them put meat on the menu.

Approaching the main entrance from the street, you arrive at their door beneath the elegance of a fringed gold canopy.

Upon entering, one is immediately captivated by the large aquarium, the many interesting pictures on the walls and the unusual tables. Made from cable wire reels, they have been joined together by an attractive circle of heavy rope and finished off with an epoxy resin.

The fare is excellent, with a good choice for "living" food fans.

Only one word would describe the "Fresh Fruit" plate that Chris' daughter, Boots, ordered, "Magnificent!" As the waiter, Allan, delivered it, he reassured her with, "When you are ready, I'll bag the rest of it for you." (The bag turned out to be a very attractive plastic tray with a hinged lid which enabled them to make a work of art out of what she took home.)

At one point, when some guests were leaving, an aristocratic visitor raced in through the front door. Four white socks and an outstanding white mustache marked this long fluffy-haired black and white "Super Tom." A regular visitor, we soon learned, he knew good food when he saw it and was exceptionally fond of fruit.

Something to please everyone was found here.

*THE MAGIC APPLE INN* recommends their:

 **RAW VEGETABLE SALAD**

| | |
|---|---|
| Red leaf lettuce | Alfalfa sprouts |
| Romaine lettuce | Cherry tomatoes |
| Cauliflower sections | Grated carrots |
| Broccoli sections | Grated zucchini |
| Sliced cucumber | Grated beets |
| Sliced mushrooms | |

On a bed of romaine lettuce, layer bite size red leaf lettuce. Layer next a mound of alfalfa sprouts. Attractively place cauliflower sections, small broccoli sections, sliced cucumbers, sliced mushrooms and cherry tomatoes. Top with 3 mounds of string grated carrots, zucchini, and beets.

Serve with your favorite herb dressing. (The Magic Apple turned down our request for theirs, a top secret.)

Whole grain sesame rolls, or poppy seed rolls make a welcome addition.

## THE AWARE INN - 8828 Sunset Blvd.
## Los Angeles, CA.

Sophisticated with a New York air about it would be a good description of the Aware Inn.

Greeted by a hostess in a formal gown, surrounded by waiters in white jackets and black ties, one is soon aware that there are two white tablecloths on every table.

Atmosphere is first created by a heavy wood arched entrance doorway. This opens to expose an unusually arched ceilinged room which has been played up by using decorator's wallpaper, a kind of wild but dignified rose red background with a grayed green silver design reflecting the lights with a sequined effect.

Old world flavor is introduced by mahogany booths, stained glass window above wooden shutters, cut glass room divider, round ice cream parlor lamps, and a real fire in the fireplace.

In the upstairs dining room the red theme is climaxed by the red velvet draped picture window overlooking the many lights of Los Angeles.

According to Alta, the manager hostess, the owner, Elaine Baker, looks upon her restaurant as a service to mankind, making people more aware of the proper food for their bodies.

### THE AWARE INN recommends their:

### SPINACH AND MUSHROOM SALAD

| | |
|---|---|
| **Olive oil** | **Sesame seeds** |
| **Vinegar** | **Tender spinach leaves** |
| **Herbs** | **Sliced raw mushrooms** |
| **Lemon juice** | |

Line your plate with tender spinach leaves. Pile on a generous portion of sliced raw mushrooms. Combine olive oil, vinegar, lemon juice and herbs and pour over the top of the salad. Sprinkle with sesame seeds.

*JAY'S CAFE* - Mission Blvd., Pacific Beach, CA

How does one become the owner of a Vegetarian Restaurant? And an adjoining Farmer's Market?

Jay Gordon planned on spending the winter of '76-'77 playing tennis tournaments. Then he hurt his knee.

Having just sold a successful Jay's Cafe in El Cajon, California in order that he might play tennis, Jay headed for Hawaii and only got as far as the oceanfront of San Diego. An irresistable opportunity to buy a restaurant, market combination on Garnet Avenue, Pacific Beach, kept him in California instead.

Jay is originally from Beaver Falls, Pennsylvania, where he used to play in the same Little League with Joe Namath. However, when Eydie Mae and Chris interviewed Jay, his claim to fame came (when it was discovered) from the fact that he had been taught in first grade by Dorothy Loeffler, Chris' Aunt by marriage. Aunt "Dick", as she was affectionately known by the family, taught first grade in the same school for forty years in Beaver Falls, Pennsylvania.

The majority of people are a real disappointment to Jay because they "couldn't care less" for learning about better eating habits. He claims that the organic foods in the market go largely untouched by customers. The organic foods get used in his restaurant, Jay's Cafe.

White cafe curtains grace the windows in the dining room, while antique looking tables and chairs beckon you to sit down and enjoy good conversation while trying a "Joyburger", or "Eggplant Elegant". Hanging plants complete the cheerful atmosphere, and the service is good.

 **JAY'S CAFE DRESSING**

3 cups safflower oil
1 cup fresh lemon juice
2 cloves garlic
⅓ cup tamari soy sauce
⅓ cup water

½ cup sesame seeds
2 T. parsley, chopped fine
1 T. dill weed, chopped fine
2 tsp. oregano
1 tsp. basil

Shake well before using.

### *MOTHER'S KITCHEN* - 2721 East Coast Highway, Corona Del Mar, CA.

"Forty people came in when we opened the doors! We've been in the black from day one," announced Kanti, our waitress at Mother's Kitchen.

Steven Connella is the owner of this one and one half year old health food restaurant where about 25 young people are employed.

Kanti relayed the fact that they are 99% vegetarian. She replied with conviction, "I have a lot more energy and feel more alive. Meat meals used to weigh me down. There are spiritual advantages also. The body is the temple where the Lord resides. I want to keep it pure."

The name, "Mother's Kitchen" creates their atmosphere, and they have followed through on the theme all the way. Shelves hold plants just above your head; hanging plants grace the corners. Large panelled framed mirrors open up the area which seats around 28. A canopy over the kitchen entrance is shrouded in calico, draping ruffled calico curtains to the floor, through which calico aproned waitresses disappear and reappear with delightful food prepared to order, served on tables graced by fresh flowers in calico covered vases.

My mother never did, but at Mother's Kitchen they grind their own wheat every morning to make their own bread. Their ice cream is homemade, and every day they have a special.

In the patio area of the arcade adjacent to the restaurant, there is outside seating creating the air of a sidewalk cafe. There were even a few brave souls seated outside on that cool November evening.

Don't miss their raw fruit pie, a recipe originating in Mother's Kitchen.

### RAW APPLE PIE
from Mother's Kitchen

2 cups shredded coconut                1 cup of ground walnuts
1 lb. of date pieces                   ½ cup grated apples

Mix together well and press into pie shell. Grate apples to fill the shell generously.

2½ tsp. cinnamon                       Apple juice
Raisins

Blend in the blender ½ cup grated apples with a small amount of apple juice and cinnamon. Mix well with grated apples and put in pie crust. Refrigerate for 1 hour. Serve cool.

### MOTHER'S GARDEN SALAD
from Mother's Kitchen

3 handfuls of torn romaine lettuce     3 sliced mushrooms
1 handful grated zuchinni              4 cucumber slices
1 handful grated carrots               2 scoops of avocado
½ handful bean sprouts                 Raw sunflower seeds, raw
                                           cashews, and raw almonds

Mix all together, serving with Herb dressing (following). Garnish with the sliced mushrooms, sunflower seeds, cashews and almonds.

### HERB DRESSING
from Mother's Kitchen

To make 1 pitcher full
⅔ c. apple cider vinegar               1 handful parsley
2 lemons, juiced                       ¼ tsp. red cayenne pepper
2⅓ cups sesame oil                         (a Chris substitute for 1 tsp
1 stalk celery                             white pepper)
1 bell pepper                          1 tsp. thyme
2 tsp. vegetable salt                  1 tsp. paprika

Blend all in the blender.

## NATURAL FOODS RESTAURANT GUIDES

When we travel, we have found the following two books to be an enormous help in finding restaurants that specialize in natural foods:

*THE ORGANIC TRAVELER* by Maxine Davis and Gregory J. Tetrault, Grasshopper Press, Diamond Lake Station, P.O. Box 19053, Minneapolis, Minnesota 55419.

*THE EXCITING WORLD OF NATURAL FOODS AND VEGETARIAN RESTAURANTS IN SOUTHERN CALIFORNIA* by Ivy Shorr, Dennis - Landman Publisher, Santa Monica, California.

**CHAPTER II.**

 **BAHAMA DELIGHT**

**1 coconut**

To open the coconut take a screwdriver and find the "soft" eye out of the three eyes at the end of the coconut. Poke it out and drain the milk. Place coconut into a plastic bag and whack it good with a hammer. All the pieces end up neatly inside the bag. Enjoy the fresh coconut milk. Break the flesh to the coconut into small pieces, grind to a powder and place in blender with small amount of water, or cut up into small pieces and gradually add to the water while blender is in motion. Blend until it is changed into a milk-like liquid.

 **FERMENTED BEETS IN JUICE**

**Beets (enough to fill your crock)**     **Cheesecloth**

Wash beets, peel and cut into quarters. Place in crock and cover with water. Cover crock with cheesecloth and let stand at room temperature 1 wk. Uncover and remove scum. Stir and recover. Let stand 2 or 3 wks., until liquid is scarlet and clear.

 **FRUIT DRINKS**

 **Any fresh fruit**

Put through your juicer or juice extractor, or blend cut up fruit in blender. Use a little bit of water if needed in your blender. Strain if desired.

 **THE GREEN COCKTAIL**

1 qt. of carrot juice
1 stalk of celery, juiced
1 fresh tomato

8 oz. of wheat grass juice
Several sprigs of parsley
Kelp to taste

Blend together all ingredients in your blender. Drink immediately. Serves 6.

Wheat grass is not compatible with fruits. Wait one hour after fruit or fruit juice is taken before taking wheat grass juice. All meals other than fruit may be taken immediately or shortly after your wheat grass cocktail. Never take wheat grass juice right after a meal.

 **IMITATION BUTTER-MILK**

½ oz. flax-seed                     6 oz. water

Liquefy in blender. Blend every 10 minutes for one hour.

¾ oz. lemon juice (3 T.)          1 oz. pignolias (pine nuts)

Grind pignolias. Mix well with lemon juice. Let stand 15 minutes. Add to flax-seed mixture and liquefy. Some prefer this strained.

 **NUTRI MILK**

1 pint water
1 rounded T. sesame meal
   (ground sesame seed)
1 rounded tsp. sunflower seeds

1 rounded T. pepitas
   (pumpkin seeds)
2 T. chopped nuts

Put water in the blender gradually adding dry ingredients to water. When well blended, add one part nut milk to 2 parts carrot juice. Sweeten with honey if desired.

## PINEAPPLE GRAPEFRUIT JUICE

1 fresh pineapple          1 fresh grapefruit

Put the pineapple through a juice extractor, core and all. Add to this the juice of 1 fresh grapefruit and shake. Serve chilled, it makes a nice party drink.

## REJUVELAC

1 cup soft spring wheat       3 cups water

Cover wheat berries with water and soak 24 hrs. Pour off the water which is ready to drink or use in your favorite recipe. Refrigerate any excess. Put 3 more cups of water on wheat and repeat. This may be done about 3-4 times. You can then blend the soaked wheat for a cheese if you choose. It will not sprout for wheat grass. It can also be used as worm feed, or as a fertilizer on your plants.

## SESAME SEED DRINK
from Hazel Richards - Hippocrates Health Institute, Boston.

½ cup sesame seeds       6 pitted dates - soaked
¹/₈ T. kelp powder        1½ cups water

Blend all in your blender until smooth.
This drink has protein and minerals and 10 times more calcium than milk.

Sat Kartar and Sat Tirath, formerly of Hippocrates Health Institute in San Diego recommend *BLENDED SMOOTHIES:*

## DELICIOUS TROPICAL YOGI

Equal parts banana, papaya, with six dates (preferrably pre-soaked). Blend.

## GRAPE WHAMMY

1 cup of organic grape juice          1 banana

Blend well.

## MANGO MANIA

1 large mango                6 fresh apricots (or soaked
1 papaya                        dried apricots)

Peel the mango and the papaya. Blend all three together.

## YUCATAN YUMMY

1 cup fresh orange juice          ⅓ of a fresh coconut
1 cup fresh chopped pineapple

Blend well.

## B-BONGO

1 cup apple juice          4 fresh or soaked dried figs
1 fresh peach

Blend well.

## *MORE SMOOTHIES:*

## FALL SPECIAL

1 cup fresh apple juice          1 juicy pear

Blend well.

## VITAMIN "C" SPECIAL

1 cup fresh pineapple          1 cup fresh orange or
                                grapefruit juice

Blend well.

## TROPICAL SPECIAL

1 mango                    1 papaya, cut up
1 banana                   ½ cup water

Pour water in blender. Add banana, papaya and mango while blender is in motion. Add more water if desired. Makes a delicious enzyme filled drink.

 **VEGETABLE COCKTAIL**

Combine and blend your favorite vegetables in a juicer or juice extractor. Combinations are endless. A pleasing drink is:

| | |
|---|---|
| **#1.** **Carrot and celery** | **#3.** **Tomato and parsley** |
| **#2.** **Carrot, celery, and parsley** | **#4.** **Red Potato** |

 **VEGETABLE COCKTAIL**

1½ cups tomato, chopped
1 large stalk celery, chopped
1 small onion, sliced

1 small carrot, diced
1 or 2 sprigs parsley
Dill

Mix well and chill.

 **WHEAT GRASS COCKTAIL**

*First day*

1 T. wheat grass chlorophyll juice
4 oz. of Rejuvelac
Mix together and drink.

*After the second day—*
increase gradually to:

2 oz. wheat grass chlorophyll juice
6 oz. Rejuvelac
Mix together and drink.

## *SOME LETTERS FROM LIVE FOODS FANS*

I have MS and I find that I fare better to stay on raw, live foods. I am not able to get wheatgrass here so I buy "Wachter Organic Sea Food - liquid chlorophyll" and take a teaspoon in a glass of rejuvelac once a day... I am tolerating this Arizona heat so much better this year and have more energy just by this diet.

L.O., Mesa, AZ

I know the merits of Eydie Mae's program because I have been on a similar program for arthritis for over four years now. I use basically natural raw foods together with the colonic cleansing. A big thank you to Eydie Mae for sharing her experiences and knowledge with others. And three cheers for Arn.

T.S., Santa Ana, CA

**CHAPTER III.**

# AVOCADO
# STUFFED CELERY

| | |
|---|---|
| 1 avocado | Sweet pepper |
| 2 onion slices, chopped fine | Powdered herbs or |
| | vegetable seasoning |

Mash avocado. Combined with onion and seasoning. Stuff celery stalks and serve.

## CELERY STICKS

| | |
|---|---|
| Celery | Sesame butter |
| Nut butter | Sunflower butter |

Stuff celery stalks cut in 6 inch lengths with nut butter, some with sesame butter, and some with sunflower butter.

## NUT STUFFED CELERY

| | |
|---|---|
| Celery stalks (2) | 1 tsp. wheat germ |
| 2 T. organic almond butter | $^1/_8$ tsp. sea salt |
| 1 T. sunflower seeds, ground | Lemon juice (if need thinning) |

Rinse and dry celery. Mix together the rest of the ingredients. Stuff into celery. Sprinkle with sesame seeds. Chill and serve cold.

 **STUFFED CELERY**

**Inside stalks of celery**          **Almond butter**

Cut the celery in four-inch lengths and lay in cold water until required, to make crisp and firm. Drain, wipe dry and fill with almond butter.

 **PLATTER VEGETABLE SALAD
or PICKIN' SALAD**

**Celery stalks, some stuffed,
  some plain
Cucumber slices or strips
Carrot sticks
Tomato wedges or slices
Cauliflowerets**

**Young green onions or
  sliced onions
Young radishes
Sweet pepper strips or rings
Rutabaga strips or rounds**

Let each select and combine the salad of his choice. Pass dressing separately if desired. Nut butters and creams make good dips and toppings.

 **VEGETABLE GARNISHES**

**Celery leaves
Lettuce leaves
Radishes
Celery curls
Carrot curls**

**Cauliflowerets
Strips of green or red pepper
Tomato
Sliced cucumber with a fancy
  green edge (If peel is
  not waxed)**

Most vegetable salads need garnishing. Add any one or more of the above garnishes to the top of the salad just before serving.

## SOME LETTERS FROM LIVE FOODS FANS

My husband and I have had the wonderful general health benefits from following the Living Foods diet with the wheat grass therapy. The doctor I have had for arthritis saw me Jan. 4. He was pleased that I had no pain or swelling and that I had stopped the medication he had prescribed for me.

G. & M. T., Irvine, CA

**CHAPTER IV.**

## ARAB POCKET BREAD

3 cups warm water
  (about 110 degrees)
1 pkg. active dry yeast
5 cups unbleached white flour
3½ cups whole wheat flour
1 T. kelp

½ cup wheat germ
1 T. salad oil
3 torn pieces of old sheet
A plastic garment bag
A large bath towel

Add yeast to the water. Allow to stand 5 minutes. Measure your 9 cups of unsifted flour into a large bowl. Add wheat germ. Make well in center and add kelp and salad oil. Add yeast mixture half at a time, mixing with your hand. Mix and knead well until flour and liquid hold together. Turn out onto well-floured board. Work into shape of a log. Divide log in half; cut into 10 equal pieces. Cover remaining log with clear plastic. Knead each piece individually by flouring the palm of your hand, pull away from sides, press in center; work around edge until smooth, elastic. Place smooth side up on cloth-lined tray. Cover with dry cloth, then damp cloth, let rise until puffy (1 - 1½ hrs.). Flatten each ball onto a floured board. Roll out from the center with 4 strokes each way to a 6 inch round. Shake off excess flour and place rounds at least ½ inch apart on dry cloth. Cover with dry cloth, then damp cloth. Cover all with plastic; let rest 1 hour until slightly puffy.

Gently lift and place 3 to 5 loaves on an ungreased cooky pan, ½ inch apart. Bake at 475 degrees in oven 2 inches from bottom until pocket forms and bottoms brown lightly, about 4 - 6 minutes. Move pan to within 4 inches from the broiler unit. Bake until tops are lightly browned, about 1 minute. Don't overbake. Cool on bath towel; wrap and store airtight.

### ESSENE BREAD

Wheat berries
Parsley, chopped fine
Celery chopped fine
Onion, chopped fine

Green pepper, chopped fine
Carrots, minced
Caraway seeds
Poppy seeds

Soak wheat berries in water 15 hours. Pour water off and allow wheat to sit until sprouted.

Put sprouted wheat through Champion juicer, vegetable chopper, or meat grinder.

Add seasonings and vegetables. Form into loaf or patties.

Bake in sun or warm place (70-90 degrees) until firm. It may be necessary to turn these a few times so that the under side does not get sticky. "Bake" about 12-24 hours. The longer they sit the more the flavors go throughout the bread.

Variation: Use raisins and dates instead of vegetables.

 **HUNZA BREAD**

| | |
|---|---|
| **5 parts whole wheat flour** | **1 part barley** |
| **1 part rye** | **1 part buckwheat groats** |
| **1 part oats** | **1 part millet** |

Grind the seeds to flour if necessary. Mix all ingredients well. Add enough water to make a medium dough. Take a ball of dough about the size of an orange and flatten in hands to 5" diameter and ¾" thick. Print with fork (Important to keep it from exploding in the oven) and bake at 350 degrees for 30-40 minutes.

 **NUT MUFFINS OR BALLS**

| | |
|---|---|
| **4 oz. ground almonds** | **4 oz. ground sunflower seeds** |
| **Safflower oil** | **2 oz. lemon juice** |

Drop a few drops of safflower oil into almonds as you grind them to butter consistency. Add to sunflower seed meal and lemon juice; knead to dough. Press into small muffin tins or roll into balls for snacks.

## TORTILLAS

**2 cups masa harina**               **1½ c. warm water**

Mix masa harina with warm water to make a stiff dough. Let stand 1 hr. Form into balls about 2 inches in diameter and roll between sheets of plastic into round thin pancakes about 6 inches in diameter. Cook on a moderately hot, dry or very lightly oiled griddle, turning frequently until dry and lightly sprinkled with brown. (The Mexicans like the white sweet corn instead of the yellow corn.)

## WAYFARER BREAD

Rinse sprouted grain and dry at least 2 hrs. Run through a meat grinder and shape into small loaves. Wrap in foil or roasting bags and bake at 200 degrees for 5 hours or 250 degrees for 3 hours.

**CHAPTER V.**

 **AVOCADO SOUP**

1 avocado
2 tomatoes
2 cups of water
2 cups of tomato juice
1 carrot
1 small clove garlic

2 stalks of celery
1 green onion
1 tsp vegetable broth
   seasoning
Dulse

Place the water and tomato juice in your blender. Add your vegetables in small pieces and liquefy in blender until smooth. Add seasoning. Garnish with chopped parsley.

 **BORSCHT**

4 cups fermented beet juice
   (see Beverages)
1 c. of beets from crock,
   sliced or chopped

1 T. kelp
Juice of 1 fresh lemon
1 medium onion, grated fine

Combine all and chill. Garnish with grated potato, parsley or chopped cucumbers and serve.

 **BUFFET SOUP**

Vegetable seasoning
Hot water
Sesame sauce
Chopped tomato

Grated carrots
Grated onions
Favorite sprouts
Bits of cucumber

Blend vegetable seasoning, hot water and sesame sauce. Add vegetables to broth and serve. Or serve vegetables in separate bowls and let each person select the vegetables to add to his individual bowl of broth. Garnish with bits of cucumber.

 **CHILI**

1 lb. pinto beans - sprouted
   3-4 days and cooked slowly
   over low heat
4-6 cups of tomatoes that have
   been put through a food grinder
1 lg. jalapeno pepper put
   through a food grinder

2 cloves of garlic put through
   a food grinder
Kelp to taste
Vegetable seasoning to taste
Oregano to taste
Chili powder to taste
1 med. onion put through
   a food grinder

Just before serving add the hot beans to the raw vegetables with enough liquid to make the right consistency. The chili will be warm to the taste.

 **CREAM OF
SWEET CORN SOUP**

2 oz. young sweet corn
   pulp grated off the cob
1 oz. pignolias, ground
   (pine nuts)

5 oz. cucumber or tomato
   juice
½ oz. parsley or celery, minced

Beat all together. Let stand half hour before serving.

 **CORN CHOWDER**

2 cups of fresh corn cut off
   the cob, or 1 pkg. frozen corn
1 green onion
1 avocado

2 cups of water
1 T. vegetable broth powder
Kelp
2 cups of tomato juice

Liquefy in blender. Garnish with chopped spinach leaves.

## CORN CHOWDER #2

2 tomatoes
Fresh corn on the cob
  (uncooked)
1 cup of water

¼ c. sunflower seed sprouts
  (sprouted only as long as
  the seed)
¼ cup chopped celery

Peel your tomatoes and mash real fine. Cut your corn off the cob. Have your celery ready all chopped fine. Heat your water to no more then 120 degrees. Add vegetables to the water after taken off the stove. If desired season with vegetable seasoning. Enzymes are killed above 120 degrees. If you prefer, you can serve this cold as well. (A candy thermometer works well for determining the heat of the water.)

—Sprinkle rye sprouts into soups just before serving. They add a mouthwatering tang.

## CORN SOUP

1 cup sweet corn (freshly grated
  from the cob)
1 cup tomato pulp
1 cup tomato juice
1 cup cucumber juice

6 oz. ground nuts
Finely chopped parsley
  or thyme
1 T. olive oil

Blend together corn, tomato pulp, tomato juice, cucumber juice, ground nuts, parsley or thyme. Let stand about 15 min. Add olive oil, beat together, and serve. (Chill if desired.)

## CUCUMBER SOUP

1 cucumber
1 zucchini
1 small avocado

1 cup Rejuvelac
Fresh lime juice to taste
Vegetable seasoning and
  garlic to taste

Blend all ingredients together to a soup consistency. Good on a hot day.

## GAZPACHO
A Chilled Mexican Soup—GOOD!

| | |
|---|---|
| **Fresh tomatoes** | **¼ c. olive oil (cold pressed)** |
| **1 large cucumber** | **¼ c. vinegar (apple cider)** |
| **1 large onion, peeled** | **1 chili pepper (I like the** |
| **or green onions** | **Floral Gem)** |
| **1 bell pepper** | **Kelp** |
| **1 can pimiento** | **Garlic** |
| **or three fresh** | **Vegetable seasoning** |
| **1 can sliced ripe olives** | |

Put tomatoes in blender and puree to make about 18 oz.-20 oz. Cut cucumber, onion, peppers, into cubes. Put in blender, add pimiento, kelp, garlic chopped fine, and seasoning, oil and vinegar and puree. Chill at least 3 hours. Also chill 6 serving bowls and a soup tureen.

Chop fresh tomato, cucumber, onion, green pepper. Place in separate bowls. Chill olives in small bowl. Sprinkle over top of each serving.

 **GREEN SOUP**

(Sopa Verde)

| | |
|---|---|
| **1 bunch green onions** | **4 cups water** |
| **2 cups shredded lettuce** | **¾ tsp kelp** |
| **4 sprigs parsley** | **1 sm. hot pepper if you like it** |
| **1 avocado** | **hot (Eydie and Chris do.)** |
| | **(Floral Gem or chili)** |

Blend all vegetables in small amount of water, gradually adding the 4 cups and kelp. Serve with warm tortillas. (For II & III.)

 **LENTIL SOUP**

| | |
|---|---|
| 1 cup slightly sprouted lentils | ½ cup chopped celery |
| 1 large onion | ½ cup parsley |
| 2 cups water | ½ tsp. veg. oil |
| 1 med. uncooked potato, diced | Kelp and vegetable seasoning |
| ½ tsp. sweet basil | to taste |

Blend together water, lentil sprouts, onions, celery, parsley, oil, sweet basil. Top with diced potato, kelp, and veg. seasoning to taste.

 **MINESTRONE**

| | |
|---|---|
| 1 clove garlic | ¼ small cabbage, shredded |
| 1 onion, minced | 2 zucchinis, diced |
| 1 leek, diced | Kelp |
| 1 T. chopped parsley | Vegetable seasoning to taste |
| 1 tsp. thyme | Sprouted garbanzas, or 2 cups |
| 4 tomatoes, chopped | cooked and drained beans |
| 3 celery stalks, chopped | ⅓ cup cooked brown rice |
| 2 carrots, diced | Water as needed for |
| 2 potatoes, diced | consistency |

**CREAM OF PEA SOUP**

| | |
|---|---|
| 5 oz. cucumber juice or | 1 oz. tender fresh green |
| tomato juice plus pulp | peas, ground |
| 1 oz. pignolias, ground | 1 T. ground wheat sprouts |
| (pine nuts) | ¼ oz. parsley, minced |

Mix together and serve.

## PEA SOUP

2 cups sprouted peas
1 green onion
1 large tomato
1 stalk celery

1 avocado
2 T. vegetable broth powder
3 cups of water
Kelp or dulse to taste

Blend together until smooth.

## POTATO SOUP

3 raw potatoes, scrubbed
   not peeled, cut up
Rejuvelac

½ avocado cut in small pieces
Vegetable seasoning
Mung bean sprouts

Blend in blender the potatoes and twice as much Rejuvelac as potatoes. Season with vegetable seasoning. Garnish with mung bean sprouts and avocado pieces.

*GOURMET SPECIALITIES* from Jon, formerly at
Hippocrates Health Institute, Boston

## TOMATO SOUP

Tomatoes
1 bell pepper
Garlic
3 drops olive oil

Lime juice
Rejuvelac
Veg.-All

Blend well.

## TOMATO VEGETABLE SOUP

1½ c. freshly chopped tomatoes
3 cups finely chopped celery
3 cups grated carrots
1 tsp. kelp

1 c. parsley, chopped fine
(save 2 T.)
¼ c. green onion, chopped
fine

Blend all together except 2 T. parsley to sprinkle on top with sprouts if desired. Add Rejuvelac or water to desired soup consistency. (This makes a delicious vegetable juice by adding another quart of water and straining.)

## CREAM OF TOMATO SOUP

6 or 8 tomatoes
6 oz. sunflower seeds

Parsley
Herbs

Peel tomatoes, cut them into pieces and macerate with a silver fork. Add seeds, flavor with parsley or other herbs, and add 2 T. olive oil. Blend in blender.

## MINCED TOMATO SOUP

6½ oz. tomatoes, chopped fine
½ oz. parsley or celery
minced very fine

1 T. ground wheat sprouts

Mix together well and serve.

## CREAM OF TOMATO SOUP

6 oz. tomatoes, chopped fine
1 oz. pignolias, ground
(pine nuts)

½ oz. celery, minced
1 tsp. olive oil

Mix together well and serve.

## VEGETABLE SOUP #1

**Rejuvelac**                                      **Corn and/or tomatoes**

Blend with Rejuvelac to a thin sauce. This is you base. Add:

**1 red pepper, chopped fine**          **2 stalks celery, diced**
**2-3 tomatoes, chopped**               **1 cup corn cut fresh**
**1 cup green peas**                        **from the cob**

Season with: **Kelp and vegetable seasoning**

## VEGETABLE SOUP #2

**1 cup fresh corn or tomatoes**        **1 cup fresh peas**
**½ red sweet pepper**                     **½ cup celery**
**1 tomato**                                   **2 green onions (optional)**

Liquefy in blender the corn or tomatoes. Chop fine the other ingredients and add to this. Season with kelp and vegetable seasoning. Garnish with parsley or ripe olives.

## VEGETABLE SOUP #3

**2 cups sprouted peas**                  **1 tomato, chopped fine**
**2 cups sprouted mung beans**         **6 cups of tomato juice**
**3 celery stalks, chopped fine**         **1 small onion, chopped fine**
**2 carrots, grated**

Stir together. Garnish with chopped parsley. Season with kelp.

**VEGETABLE SOUP #4**

**3 carrots, grated**                    **2 T. olive oil**
**2 cups fresh peas**                    **Rejuvelac or water**
**Several stalks of celery**            **Kelp and veg. seasoning**

Blend in blender and season with kelp and veg. seasoning to taste. Add Rejuvelac or water to the desired soup consistency. Top with sprouts if desired.

SALAd A-L

**CHAPTER VI.**

## SLICED APPLE SALAD

**Fresh red apples**                                   **Nut butter**

Slice your apples in a manner that you can put them together sandwich style with any good nut butter in between.

Arrange on an attractive plate garnished with lettuce leaves and celery hearts.

 ## ARMENIAN SALAD

4 lg. tomatoes, peeled and cubed    ¼ c. chopped parsley
2 cucumbers, diced    Pinch of basil, dried mint, or
2 stalks celery, sliced    1 tsp. fresh mint
½ c. finely chopped onion (red)    ¼ c. lemon juice
½ bunch watercress, chopped    2 T. cold pressed oil
2 tsp. veg. seasoning    Ground kelp to taste

Combine tomatoes, cucumbers, celery, onion, watercress, parsley, basil and mint, then toss. Sprinkle with lemon juice, oil, vegetable seasoning and kelp & toss. Many times we use just lemon juice, kelp and vegetable seasoning without oil.

 ## ASPARAGUS BOUQUET

1 green pepper    8 asparagus tips
1 cucumber    2½ cups shredded lettuce
2 stalks of tender celery

Wash the pepper and cut crosswise to make 4 small rings. Cut your cucumber and celery into 8 3-in. strips. Allow 2 strips of cucumber and celery and 2 asparagus tips to each person. Place in the pepper rings. Stand upright in lettuce nests and serve with lemon dressing.

## ASPARAGUS SALAD

2 cups chopped asparagus          1 tsp. ground sesame seed

Mix together. Place in lettuce cup. Top with salad dressing of your choice.

## AVOCADO BOAT
(one per person)

½ avocado                    Alfalfa sprouts
½ carrot, shredded           Or lettuce
1 T. chopped onion           Parsley
1 T. chopped celery          Ripe olives

Place avocado half on bed of sprouts or lettuce. Mix the carrots, onions, and celery with your favorite dressing. Fill the avocado. Garnish with parsley and ripe olives.

## BANANA CANDLE

Lettuce                          Chopped nuts
1 slice fresh pineapple per person    ½ banana per person
1 brazil nut per person          Red grapes

On a bed of lettuce, place 1 slice (round) of pineapple that has had the core removed. Place ½ banana upright, pointed end up, in hole of pineapple. Cut the brazil nut in half lengthwise and sharpen one end with a knife; stick other end into the banana. (top)

Garnish the pineapple with chopped nuts and a few red grapes. When ready to serve, light the brazil nut. It will burn because of its rich oil.

 ## BANANA NUT BUTTER SALAD

Lettuce                          Mayonnaise
1 banana                         Chopped nuts
Nut butter

On a bed of lettuce place ½ a banana sliced lengthwise. Spread with nut butter, top with 2nd half of banana. Garnish with mayonnaise and nuts.

 **BEAN SALAD**

| | |
|---|---|
| 1 c. sprouted garbanzo beans | 1 thinly sliced sweet onion |
| 1 c. pressure sprouted mung beans | 1 fresh pimiento pepper or |
| 1 c. fresh green beans, cut in pieces | 1 red bell pepper |
| 1 T. kelp | |

Toss together lightly with lemon-oil dressing and serve on bed of lettuce.

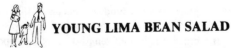 **BEAN SPROUTS SALAD**

| | |
|---|---|
| 2 T. olive oil | 1 tsp. grated fresh ginger |
| 1 green onion, chopped | ½ cup sliced mushrooms |
| 1 clove garlic, minced | ½ cup chopped walnuts |
| 4 c. bean sprouts, | 1 T. tamari sauce or |
| chopped bite size | lemon juice and kelp |

Mix all together well.

 **YOUNG LIMA BEAN SALAD**

| | |
|---|---|
| 1 oz. fresh young lima beans, | 2 oz. tomatos, chopped |
| chopped | ½ oz. almonds, chopped fine |
| 1 oz. zucchini squash, chopped | 1 oz. bell pepper, chopped fine |

Toss lightly with salad dressing and serve.

 **BEET SALAD**

| | |
|---|---|
| Shredded beet | Green onion |
| Tomatoes, chopped or | |
| cherry tomatoes, halved | |

Toss with the following dressing:

6 T. sesame oil
¼ cup lemon juice

½ T. cider vinegar
Kelp to season

 **BELL PEPPER SPECIAL**

6 green bell peppers
8 tomatoes
2 large onions
1 c. vinegar or lemon juice

1 tsp. kelp
1 tsp. paprika
½ cup oil

Cut peppers into thin strips. Cut tomato into wedges. Peel onions and chop fine. Combine peppers, tomatoes and onions in salad bowl. Mix together vinegar or lemon juice with kelp, and paprika. Beat with oil. Add dressing to vegetables and mix well. Cover and chill 2 hrs. Drain vegetables and serve.

**CABBAGE SALAD**

2 c. chopped cabbage
½ c. chopped celery
1 c. chopped Spanish onions
1 c. coarsely chopped pecans

Lettuce leaves
Olive oil
Lemon juice

Mix together the chopped cabbage, celery, onion, and pecans with equal parts of lemon juice and olive oil. Serve on lettuce leaves

 **CABBAGE SLAW**

Cabbage
Turnip

Zucchini

Grate all vegetables. A sauce made of zucchini, tiny bit of avocado, Rejuvelac, lemon juice, garlic, and Veg-All. Mix well.

## RED CABBAGE TOSS

| | |
|---|---|
| 2 c. thinly sliced red cabbage | 2 T. finely chopped onion |
| 1 c. sliced raw cauliflowerets | 3 T. apple cider vinegar |
| ½ cup chopped celery | 1 tsp. kelp |
| ⅓ c. chopped green pepper | ⅓ cup vegetable oil |

Combine cabbage, cauliflowerets, celery, pepper and onion in a bowl; toss well. Measure kelp into a jar. Add vinegar and then oil. Cover and shake vigorously to blend. Pour dressing over vegetables; toss well. Chill. Serves 4 to 5.

## CARROT SALAD

| | |
|---|---|
| Raw carrots | Lettuce leaves |
| Pine nuts | Lemon |

Grate raw carrots, mix with pine nuts or sprinkle with ground almonds. Serve on lettuce leaves with a section of lemon.

## CARROT AND PEPPER SALAD

| | |
|---|---|
| 1 oz. carrot, grated | ½ oz. radish, chopped fine |
| 1 oz. sweet pepper, grated | 1 oz. zucchini squash, chopped |
| ½ oz. parsley or celery, chopped fine | 1 oz. pignolias, ground |

Mix well and serve.

 **CAULIFLOWER SALAD #1**

| | |
|---|---|
| **Cauliflower** | **Carrot** |
| **Red pepper** | **Almonds** |
| **Tomatoes** | **Coconut** |
| **Parsley** | |

Shred cauliflower with a fine knife. Cut up red pepper and tomatoes in small pieces, add to cauliflower. (Also parsley cut up fine if desired.) Make a sauce with 1 part carrot to 1 part almonds or coconut by blending together. Use on cauliflower salad.

 **CAULIFLOWER SALAD #2**

| | |
|---|---|
| **2 cups thinly sliced raw cauliflower** | **4½ T. salad or olive oil** |
| **½ c. chopped pitted ripe olives** | **1½ T. lemon juice (fresh)** |
| **⅓ c. finely chopped green pepper** | **1½ T. apple cider vinegar** |
| **¼ c. chopped fresh pimiento or bell pepper** | **3 T. chopped onion** |
| | **1 tsp. kelp** |

In a medium bowl, combine cauliflower, olives, green pepper, pimiento and onion. In a small bowl, combine salad oil, lemon juice, vinegar and kelp; beat with rotary beater until well blended. Pour over cauliflower mixture. Refrigerate covered until well chilled (1 hr.) Spoon into salad bowls or arrange on lettuce on individual salad plates. Makes four servings.

 **CAULIFLOWER PEPPER**

| | |
|---|---|
| **Raw cauliflowerets, sliced** | **Watercress or parsley** |
| **Chopped bell peppers** | |

Mix all ingredients and serve on a bed of greens.

 **CELERY SALAD**

1 pint of chopped celery
1 cup chopped almonds
2 T. shredded fresh pimientos
   or bell pepper

Mayonaise or seed butter
Lettuce
Tomatoes

Mix together the celery, almonds, and pimientoes with the mayonnaise. Serve on lettuce leaves, garnished with sections of tomatoes.

 **CIRCLE SALAD**

2 young carrots
2 cucumbers

12 radishes
2 or 3 small tomatoes

Slice everything very thin. Arrange in circular layers on crisp lettuce leaves or shredded cabbage. Serve with seed sauce.

 **COLACHE**

1 onion, chopped
1 c. cut green beans
1 green bell pepper, chopped

6 zucchini squash, chopped
2 large tomatoes, chopped
Corn cut from 3 ears of fresh
   corn

Season with kelp and vegetable seasoning.

 **COLE SLAW**

2 c. finely shredded white cabbage
¼ c. finely shredded green onions
½ c. finely shredded celery
1 or 2 tomatoes, chopped

1 clove of garlic, pressed
Seed sauce
Caraway seeds (few)

Toss together with seed sauce.

 **CORN SALAD**

**Fresh corn on the cob**          **Pepper**
**Tomatoes**                        **Parsley**

Slice corn to make cream style corn. Add tomatoes finely cut, chopped fine pepper and parsley. Blend some corn to make a sauce to put over it.

 **CORN AND TOMATO SALAD**

**1 oz. sweet corn (young or green)**     **2 oz. tomatoes, chopped**
**sliced off the cob**                     **1 oz. pignolias, chopped**

Toss together, garnish and serve.

 **CUBAN SALAD**

**String beans**                    **Radishes, sliced**
**Asparagus**                       **Green sweet peppers**
**Slices of onions**                **Lettuce**

Cut string beans and asparagus into bits. Shred the green peppers. Mix all together with onions and radishes. Toss with seed sauce. Serve on lettuce leaves.

**CUCUMBER SALAD WITH SAUCE**

**Cucumbers**          **Peppers**
**Tomatoes**           **Parsley**

Dice cucumbers, add cut up tomatoes, pepper and parsley.
SAUCE: Blend cucumbers, add lemon juice and small amount of oil if desired.

## STUFFED CUCUMBER

| | |
|---|---|
| Cucumbers | Shredded cabbage |
| Lettuce | Grated carrots |
| Celery | Ground nuts |

Cut medium size cucumbers in half lengthwise. Peel if the cucumbers have been waxed or sprayed. Hollow out the centers; arrange on lettuce leaves. Add chopped celery to shredded cabbage and some of the cucumber hearts. Moisten with your favorite dressing; fill the cucumber. Garnish with grated carrots.

 ## DELUXE SPROUT SALAD

| | |
|---|---|
| 1 c. of your favorite sprouts | 1 diced red pepper |
| ½ c. grated celery | Leaf lettuce |
| ½ c. diced onion | Avocado |
| ½ c. grated carrots | Tomato |

Combine the sprouts, celery, onions, carrots and red pepper. Mix thoroughly in a large bowl. Toss with fresh lemon juice, kelp and vegetable seasoning. Serve on leaf lettuce and garnish with avocado and tomato.

## EGG-PLANT AND CUCUMBER SALAD

| | |
|---|---|
| 1 oz. egg-plant, chopped | ½ oz. onion, or bell peppers, |
| 1 oz. cucumbers, cut up |     minced |
| 1 oz. nut-meats, chopped | |

Mix all together and top with tomato slices sprinkled with chopped pignolias, or top with Tomato lemon sauce.

## "FATTOUSHA"
Lebanese Salad-from Denise Ebipane of the
Natural Health Foods, 158 W. Main, El Cajon, CA.

1 Syrian bread or 2 Bible bread
   or Tortillas
3-4 tomatoes, cut in medium pieces
2-3 green onions cut in
   medium pieces
½ small white onion,
   finely chopped
1 cucumber, sliced

1 bunch parsley, cut
1 T. dry or fresh mint (to taste)
3-4 pieces garlic, crushed
Sea Salt (not for Eydie - she
   would use kelp)
2 lemons
Olive oil to taste, mixture
   should have lemony taste

Open the Syrian bread or the Bible bread in half and toast lightly
in oven. Mix the rest of the ingredients together and serve on the
open bread.

## GADO GADO — INDONESIAN VEGETABLE SALAD

3 peeled carrots, cut in matchsticks
½ lb. fresh young green beans,
   cut in thin diagonals
1 lb. fresh bean sprouts
3 medium potatoes, diced

4 c. shredded salad greens,
   (lettuce, escarole,
   some kale, some spinach)
1 tomato cut in wedges

Arrange the greens on a large platter. Arrange carrots, potatoes,
green beans, and bean sprouts in rows on greens. Garnish with tomatoes.
Serve with Sesame Seed sauce.

## GARBANZO BEAN SALAD

| | |
|---|---|
| 1 clove garlic | 1 c. sprouted garbanzo beans |
| ½ head romaine lettuce | ¼ tsp. oregano, 1 tsp. kelp |
| 1 bunch leaf or red leaf lettuce | 1 T. apple cider vinegar |
| 2 or 3 stems of fresh dill | ¼ cup olive oil |
| 2 green onions, sliced fine | |

Rub the sides of your salad bowl with fresh cut garlic. Wash and drain greens thoroughly. Break into bite-size pieces. Cut off feathery leaves of dill and discard the tough stems. Add dill, green onions, and garbanzo sprouts to greens, Sprinkle with kelp and oregano. Toss well with vinegar and oil.

## GOLDEN SALAD

| | |
|---|---|
| Lettuce leaves | Grated coconut |
| Grated carrots | Nut milk |
| Ground nuts | |

Arrange 3 lettuce leaves on each salad plate. Add enough nut milk to grated carrots to moisten; then press into small muffin cups and refrigerate. When ready to serve turn these molds onto lettuce. Top with grated nuts and serve with dressing if desired.

As a variation, top with grated coconut.

## GREEN BEAN AND CARROT SALAD

| | |
|---|---|
| 3 c. chopped green beans | 1 c. grated carrots |

Mix chopped, raw green beans and grated carrots. To with favorite sauce or dressing.

## GREEN SALAD WITH JERUSALEM ARTICHOKES

| | |
|---|---|
| **2 or 3 Jerusalem artichokes** | **½ cup oil** |
| **½ c. slivered almonds** | **¼ c. lemon juice** |
| **½ tsp. cider vinegar** | **½ tsp. kelp** |
| **¼ tsp. grated lemon peel** | **Spinach, Boston or Bibb lettuce** |

Peel and slice artichokes. Combine almonds, cider vinegar, lemon peel, oil and lemon juice and beat until well blended. Add kelp. Tear greens into salad bowl. (6 cups full.) Chill well. Add sliced artichokes to greens and enough of the almond dressing to moisten well. Toss and sprinkle with a little capsicum if you like it hot.

## GREEK SALAD SUPPER

| | |
|---|---|
| **2 medium potatoes** | **¼ bunch watercress, rinsed,** |
| **1 T. each minced parsley and** | **drained, chopped** |
| **green onion** | **2 c. shredded salad greens** |
| **1 T. salad oil (cold pressed)** | **(escarole, chicory and lettuce)** |
| **½ T. apple cider vinegar** | **1 lg. tomato, cut in wedges** |
| **Kelp and vegetable seasoning** | **½ avocado, sliced** |
| **1/8 c. mayonnaise** | **½ cucumber, cut in spears** |
| **¼ red onion, separated in rings** | **½ green pepper, seeded,** |
| **(thinly sliced)** | **sliced in rings** |
| **½ bunch radishes, cleaned** | |

Slice potatoes, toss with parsley, green onion, oil, vinegar, kelp and vegetable seasoning; add mayonaise. Chill until ready to serve. Arrange on bed of watercress and greens on platter. Mound potatoes in center and arrange tomato wedges, avocado, cucumber, green pepper, onion on greens surrounding potato salad. Have a side dish of sunflower seeds and pumpkin seeds. Have Herb dressing available.

## GUMBO SALAD

½ oz. okra pods, chopped
½ oz. parsley or celery, minced
1 oz. pignolias, ground (pine nuts)

1 oz. curled kale or chinese
  cabbage, chopped

Mix thoroughly and top with 2 oz. of chopped tomatoes.

## HADDIT SALAD

2 c. fermented seed sauce
1 c. each ground sesame and
  sunflower seed
1 c. each mung beans sprouts,
  lentil and alfalfa sprouts
1 bell pepper (red or green)

1 c. chopped parsley
5 large carrots, shredded
¼ tsp. caraway
2 tomatoes, chopped
2 stalks celery, chopped
¼ tsp. Thyme
¼ tsp. Basil

Combine fermented sesame and sunflower sauce. Add ground sesame and sunflower seed. Season with ground caraway, basil and thyme. Combine sprouts. Chop fine, tomatoes, celery, bell pepper and parsley. Shred carrots. Add all to the seasoned seed mixture. set in a warm place for 3-5 hours to integrate the herbal flavors. Decorate and serve as a main dish, or stuff peppers, celery or tomatoes.

VARIATION: Substitute sprouted chick peas (garbanzo beans) for an equal amount of seed, or use ground almonds. Remember the almonds are much richer to use accordingly. Sprout or soak the chick peas 24 hrs. and run through grinder.

## LAYERED SALAD

1 qt. salad greens
1 thinly sliced zucchini
2 c. pressure sprouted mung beans
¼ lb. sliced mushrooms

¾ c. sliced radishes
½ c. sunflower seeds
2 large tomatoes, sliced
Guacamole

Pile salad greens on plates and top with zucchini, mung beans, mushrooms, and radishes. Top with guacamole and sunflower seeds. Garnish with tomatoes.

## THE LIQUID SALAD

¾ c. finely chopped onion
¾ tsp. minced garlic
1½ c. finely chopped green pepper
3½ c. diced fresh tomatoes
1 T. kelp

1 T. paprika
1 T. olive oil
½ c. fresh lemon juice
1 c. water
½ c. thinly sliced cucumbers

Blend and chill 2-3 hrs. Add cucumber just before serving.

## LENTIL, SPINACH SALAD

1 c. sprouted lentils
2 c. chopped spinach

6 green onions, chopped

Mix and serve with favorite sauce or dressing.

## STUFFED·SWEET PEPPERS

1½ oz. sweet potato, grated
½ oz. celery, chopped fine

1 oz. pignolias, chopped
2 small bell peppers

Cut the top off the peppers, remove core and seeds. Chop the tops and the cores and mix with the grated sweet potato, celery and nuts. Toss lightly with enough mayonaise to moisten. Stuff peppers and serve.

## SOME LETTERS FROM LIVE FOODS FANS

I passed your book "How I Conquered Cancer Naturally" on to a brother who had cancer and two months to live after surgery. After going to Ann Wigmore's and getting on wheat grass, today his health is perfect and he is back to work, sometimes twelve hours a day.

F.J.K., Bath, NY

Must share my good news with you. This past Thursday I went to my doctor at Kaiser Hospital. All the thickening had disappeared and as far as the doctor could tell I was perfectly well. I heard you speak last July 4. I started the program July 5. This is March of the following year, so you see it worked for me, too. Thank you for sharing your information in your book "How I Conquered Cancer Naturally" and lecturing.

M.U., San Diego, CA

SALAd M-Z

**CHAPTER VII.**

 **MIAMI SPECIAL**

**Grapefruit**                                    **Fresh pineapple**
**Oranges**

Separate segments of grapefruit and orange from the peel and fibrous portion. Arrange on salad plates alternately, in a circle around a mound of diced fresh pineapple. Serve with your favorite dressing, or it is delicious plain.

 **MARINATED MUSHROOMS**

¼ lb. fresh mushrooms                   1 green onion, chopped
2 T. lemon juice                            Kelp to season
2 T. safflower oil

Rinse mushrooms. Mix remaining ingredients. Add mushrooms and refrigerate for 2 days. Stir occasionally. Serve cold.

 **MUSHROOM SALAD**

6 T. salad oil                                 ½ c. chopped green onions
¼ c. lemon juice                            1 tsp. kelp
½ T. cider vinegar                          1 tsp. vegetable seasoning
1 lb. fresh mushrooms, thinly sliced   Lettuce

Blend oil, lemon juice and vinegar. Toss with mushrooms, kelp, veg. seasoning, and onions. Chill. Serve on lettuce leaves torn into bite size pieces.

 **NUT CREAM SLAW**

1 oz. potato, unpeeled, sliced
  thin and chopped
1 oz. cabbage, shredded
½ oz. onion, minced

1 oz. walnut meats, chopped
½ oz. caraway seeds
2 oz. cucumber, grated

Mix all together well and serve.

 **NUT SALAD**

1 c. pecan nuts, chopped
1 c. cucumbers, chopped

Lettuce
Salad dressing

Mix together the chopped nuts and cucumbers. Mound in the center of freshly washed, crisp lettuce leaves. Serve with salad dressing. Garnish with parsley.

 **NUTSENHEIMER SALAD**

Finely chopped bronze lettuce
Chopped green onion
Finely shredded turnip
Avocado
Napa cabbage

Tomato
Almond butter or sesame seed
  or sunflower seed butter
Lemon juice

Mix almond butter with lemon juice to flavor. Spread on napa cabbage leaf about 1/8 inch thick. Toss chopped lettuce, onion and shredded turnip together. Fill cabbage leaf with this mixture. Garnish top with wedges of tomato and slices of avocado. Serve with Simple sauce.

## ORIENTAL SALAD

6 c. thinly sliced chinese cabbage    ½ c. almonds
1 c. thinly sliced radishes    Salad dressing
2 T. sesame seeds

Combine cabbage, radishes, sesame seeds and almonds in salad bowl. Toss well with salad dressing.

 ## HERB PEAS AND CORN

3 c. shelled peas    Majoram or oregano
2 c. fresh corn cut from cob    Kelp
Parsley (fresh)    Vegetable seasoning
Lemon oil dressing if desired

Mix well together.

 ## PEAS AND MUSHROOMS

1 c. fresh mushrooms,    1 small onion, thinly sliced
   thinly sliced    1 T. kelp
2 c. fresh shelled peas    Lemon oil dressing or your
     favorite sauce

Mix together and serve.

 ## PEA AND TOMATO SALAD

1 oz. fresh young peas    ½ oz. parsley, minced
1 oz. pecans, chopped fine    2 oz. tomato, chopped fine

Mix together and serve.

## PERSIMMON SALAD

**Persimmons**                    **Tokay grapes**

Arrange slices of persimmon around a mound of seeded Tokay grapes. They are usually in season together and blend deliciously.

## PICKIN' SALAD
## WITH GUACAMOLE DIP

**Celery sticks**                 **Radishes**
**Carrot sticks**                 **Sliced turnips**
**Zucchini sticks**               **Sliced beets**
**Cherry tomatoes**               **Raw broccoli slices**

On a large round platter, arrange in eight sections around the outside of the platter. Set dish of guacamole dip in the center.

## PICO DE GALLO
(Rooster's Beak) - A Crunchy Salad from Ruth Serna

**2 c. peeled, diced jicama (a**          **1 c. sliced or diced cucumber**
  **Mexican vegetable that tastes**       **¼ c. olive oil**
  **like a cross between a raw apple**    **1 green bell pepper,**
  **and a raw potato)**                     **seeded and slivered**
**½ medium mild onion,**                   **2 tsp. apple cider vinegar**
  **thinly sliced**                        **Oregano**

Mix all together lightly. Season with oregano to suit your taste. Serves from 4 - 6.

## STUFFED PIMIENTO PEPPERS

**12 fresh pimiento peppers**             **½ recipe of Mexican sauce**
  **may substitute 6 small**              **3 cups fresh corn cut**
  **bell peppers**                          **from cob**

Mix corn and sauce together and stuff peppers. Garnish with parsley or cilantro.

## PINEAPPLE SPECIAL SALAD

| | |
|---|---|
| 1 c. fresh pineapple, cut-up | 1 sour apple, cut-up |
| (& 2 round slices) | |
| ½ c. cut-up orange | 1 pomegranate |

Mix together cut-up pineapple, orange and sour apple. Arrange on top of a full round slice of fresh pineapple. Sprinkle pomegranate seeds on top.

## POTATO AND CARROT SALAD

| | |
|---|---|
| 1 carrot, grated | 1 tsp. olive oil |
| 1 med. unpeeled potato | ½ mashed avocado |
| shedded | Minced parsley, cayenne, |
| 1 tsp. chopped onion | and paprika to taste |

Mix all ingredients together. Serve in a lettuce cup. Sprinkle with dill seed, or sunflower seeds, or sesame seeds.

## JANE MURPHY'S HERB POTATO SALAD

| | |
|---|---|
| 3 med. potatoes, scrubbed | 2 T. mayonaise or enough |
| and peeled (very thin peel) | seed sauce to moisten |
| 1 med. green pepper, | Few drops of lemon juice to |
| chopped very fine | keep potatoes from |
| 1 celery stalk, chopped fine | turning dark |
| 1 med. red onion, chopped fine | Dash of kelp |
| ¼ tsp. "Italian Herbs" | Dash of cumin |
| crushed between fingers | |

Chop all the vegetables and have rest of ingredients ready to toss into salad. Grate potatoes and sprinkle on lemon juice - mix. Add rest of ingredients and gently mix. Serve at once.

## PINK POTATO SALAD

2 potatoes (do not peel)
  chopped fine
1 sm. turnip (do not peel), grated
1 carrot (do not peel), grated
1 cucumber (do not peel),
  chopped fine
Kelp

1 sm. beet (do not peel)
  grated
1 stalk celery, chopped fine
2 sm. onions (green),
  chopped fine
Minced parsley
Vegetable seasoning

Toss all together with seed sauce.

## PRUNE DELIGHT

Large, sweet, moist prunes      Fresh coconut, grated

Pit prunes. Stuff with fresh grated coconut. Arrange on lettuce. Serve with a simple dressing.
Variation: Dates can be prepared in the same way.

## RADISH SALAD

4 bunches radishes
⅓ c. thin onion rings
1 c. diced fresh tomato
1 T. kelp
1 small clove garlic

1 tsp. chopped, fresh mint
2 T. fresh lemon juice
2 T. cold pressed sesame oil
Parsley

Mix vegetables. Combine seasoning, oil and lemon juice. Pour over vegetables and toss lightly.

## SALAD PLATE

2 carrots, grated
1 med. beet, (the spinach beet
   is especially sweet), grated

½ head cabbage, shredded
1 cucumber, chopped
½ c. sweet onion, chopped fine

Make separate mounds of grated and shredded and chopped vegetables. Sprinkle with chopped onion. Serve with your favorite dressing or sauce.

## SELECTED SALAD

½ oz. carrot, chopped
½ oz. turnip or kohl-rabi,
   chopped to size of corn

1 oz. pignolias, chopped
   (pine nuts)
1 oz. sweet corn sliced off cob

   Mix all together and serve.

## SPINACH SALAD

3 T. cider vinegar
6 T. salad oil
½ tsp. kelp
¼ tsp. dry mustard
2 T. chopped parsley

1 clove garlic, cut in half
5-6 cups fresh spinach
½ cauliflower, sliced
1 avocado, sliced
½ red onion or 3 green onions

Mix together vinegar, oil, kelp, dry mustard, parsley and garlic. Let stand about 30 minutes. Remove garlic. Wash the spinach and remove stems. Put in a bowl with cauliflower, avocado and onion. Add dressing and toss lightly.

## SPINACH, MUSHROOM AND RED ONION SALAD

½ lb. mushrooms, sliced
3 T. lemon juice
⅓ c. cold pressed safflower oil
1 red onion, sliced and separated

2 c. torn spinach leaves
5 c. torn salad greens
  (red, romaine, or other)
Veg. seasoning and kelp to taste

Marinate mushrooms in combined lemon juice and oil. Toss with onion, spinach and greens, then season with veg. seasoning and kelp.

## SPINACH AND ONION SALAD

1 bunch of spinach
¼ c. sunflower or pumpkin
  seeds soaked for one hour in
  water enough to cover

1 bunch of onions
1 T. cider vinegar
1 tsp. kelp
3 T. oil

Wash and drain spinach thoroughly. Pinch off stems and any bruised leaves. Tear into bite-size pieces into a salad bowl. Slice up the bunch of onions, tops included. Blend vinegar, kelp, and oil. Toss well after adding seeds.

## SPLENDID TRIO SALAD

4 fresh figs
1 papaya, sliced lengthwise
  (peeled)

Bing cherries
2 clear glass or white salad
  plates

Arrange the fruit in three sections on the plates, piling the bing cherries high.

## SPROUT SALAD

2 c. sprouts (mung, garbonzo, lentils, either used alone or mixed)
1 c. grated carrots
½ c. chopped celery
½ tsp. kelp

½ c. sweet red bell pepper, chopped
½ c. sliced almonds
1 T. sesame seeds
¼ c. parsley or watercress

Mix and serve with the vinegar, lemon and oil dressing.

## TABOLI

2 c. cracked wheat, soaked, drained
(or sprouted wheat which is sweeter)
Chop fine:

2 lg. fresh tomatoes
1 cucumber
2 bunches green onions

1 green pepper
2 bunches parsley

Dressing:

1 c. cold pressed oil (sesame or safflower are good)

1 c. lemon juice
Kelp

Mix all together and chill.

## TABOLI MINT SALAD

1 c. sprouted wheat
1 c. minced green onion
2 c. parsley, chopped
½ c. fresh mint, chopped

1 c. tomatoes, fresh chopped
1 c. fresh lemon juice
⅓ c. cold pressed olive oil
Kelp

Serve on a bed of lettuce or may be used in Bible bread as a sandwich filling.

# GREEN TOMATO SALAD

3 oz. green tomatoes, chopped
½ oz. parsley or celery, minced

1 oz. pignolias ground with
1 tsp. olive oil

Mix all together and serve.

# GREEN TOMATO AND POTATO SALAD

1½ oz. potato or sweet potato,
    diced
1 oz. green tomato, chopped

½ oz. celery or parsley, minced
1 oz. nut meats, chopped

Mix all together and serve.

# TOMATOES STUFFED
# WITH JAPANESE CUCUMBERS

6 ripe tomatoes
1 c. olive oil
½ c. apple cider vinegar
Kelp

3 lg. Japanese cucumbers
½ c. chopped Chinese parsley
Fresh lemon juice

Carefully hollow the top quarter of whole tomatoes by removing pulp, seeds and core. Blend oil and vinegar with kelp. Pour over chopped cucumber and parsley, mix lightly and let rest in refrigerator for an hour or more. Drain well (dressing may be reserved for future salads) and stuff tomatoes with mixture. Squeeze a little fresh lemon juice over each serving and garnish with sprigs of parsley.

**TOMATO MEDLEY**

| | |
|---|---|
| 2 lg. tomatoes | Pinch of dill weed |
| 1 cucumber | 3 mint flakes or 1 tsp. minced |
| ½ c. minced parsley | fresh mint |
| ½ sm. red onion, thinly sliced, | 1 tsp. kelp |
| or 1 bunch green onions | Dash cayenne |
| 3 stalks celery, diced | Juice of 2 lemons |
| ½ bunch watercress, chopped | 2 T. oil |
| Pinch of basil | 1 tsp. apple cider vinegar |

Cut tomatoes into wedges into salad bowl. Peel and slice cucumber. Add all ingredients except last three, mix. Toss well with lemon juice, oil and vinegar.

 **TOMATO ONION SALAD**

| | |
|---|---|
| Ripe tomatoes | Bermuda onions |

Slice ripe tomatoes, not too thin, and arrange slices on a platter alternately with slices of Bermuda onion. Serve with lemon juice.

 **TOMATO SALAD**

| | |
|---|---|
| Lettuce | Minced onion |
| Quartered tomatoes (partially) | Chopped parsley |
| Thinly sliced cucumbers | |

Put on individual salad plates a layer of crisp lettuce; in the center place a small, partially quartered tomato, surrounded with a wreath of thinly sliced cucumbers. Into the center of each tomato drop 1 small teaspoon of finely minced onion, sprinkled with a pinch of chopped parsley. Serve with seed sauce.

### STUFFED TOMATO #1

**6 tomatoes**
**1 oz. pignolias, ground (pine nuts)**

**½ oz. celery, minced**
**(or parsley)**

Halve tomatoes. Cut out center pith and save for capping. Scrape out the rest of the tomato and mix with the rest. Refill the halves with this mixture. Cover with the piths reversed.

### STUFFED TOMATOES #2

**Tomatoes**
**Celery, chopped**

**Cabbage, chopped**
**Onion, minced**

Scoop out about ⅔ of tomato pulp after cutting a small slice from the top of firm tomatoes. Combine pulp with celery, cabbage and onion and your favorite dressing. Refill tomato cups and serve on lettuce. Garnish with parsley.

### STUFFED TOMATOES #3

**4 large tomatoes**
**2 stalks parsley**
**4 green onions**
**1 cucumber**

**½ green pepper**
**1/8 head cabbage**
**½ c. just sprouted wheat seeds**
**4 lettuce leaves**

Remove the centers from the tomatoes. Chop fine with the parsley, onions, cucumber, green pepper, cabbage, and wheat sprouts. Moisten well with mayonnaise. Stuff the tomato shells. Serve on a lettuce leaf with or without salad dressing.

 **FILLED TOMATO SALAD**

**Ripe tomatoes**                    **Raw potato salad**
**Fresh green peas**                   **(see salads)**

Scoop out tomatoes, fill with potato salad mixed with green peas. Serve on lettuce. Cabbage salad may be used in place of potato salad.

 **STUFFED TOMATO ROSE**

**1 tomato for each person**          **Minced onion**
**Chopped celery**

Mix together the celery and onion with your favorite dressing. Cut unpeeled tomato almost all the way through, into 6 sections. Fill the center with the chopped celery and onion mixture. Place on individual lettuce leaves.

 **TOSSED SALAD**

**Bronze leaf lettuce**                    **Fresh corn on the cob**
**Romaine lettuce also if desired**        **Cucumber**
**Bell peppers with seeds**                **Green onion**
**Jicama**                                 **Cilantro-just a sprig as it is**
**Tomatoes**                                 **strong flavored**
**Carrots**                                **Tomatillas (green Mexican**
**Celery**                                   **tomatoes)**
**Potatoes**                               **Turnip**
**Cauliflower**                            **Beet**
**Broccoli**                               **Avocado**
**Fresh peas**                             **Fresh green beans**

Tear or cut up your lettuce into bite sizes. Use your favorite vegetables. Serve with lemon juice, or apple cider vinegar and oil.

## TOSSED SALAD #2

Romaine lettuce
Red leaf lettuce
Head lettuce
Beet tops
Sliced tomatoes
Thinly sliced cauliflower

Thinly sliced cabbage (red)
Chopped bell pepper
Alfalfa sprouts
Sunflower seed sprouts
Raw grated beets
Herb dressing

Add any small pieces of raw vegetables left over from previous meals and toss with Herb dressing. Garnish with sliced radishes and raw mushrooms. Use any of your favorite vegetables as substitutes or additions.

## VARIETY GREEN SALAD

6 lg. bronze lettuce leaves
6 lg. romaine lettuce leaves
3 leaves spinach

6 leaves endive
6 leaves dandelion

Tear up in a bowl. Any other greens may be added, such as comfrey, kale, or other types of lettuce. Top with your favorite dressing. Garnish with red pepper slices or tomato slices.

## GERMAN VEGETABLE SALAD

12 stalks of asparagus
1 small cauliflower
1 stalk celery
3 medium-sized tomatoes

1 Bermuda onion
Lettuce hearts
Radishes
Cabbage leaves

Dice the asparagus, cauliflower, celery, tomatoes, and onion. Mix well with mayonnaise and serve on tender cabbage leaves. Garnish with lettuce hearts and radishes, cut in fancy shapes.

## QUICKY VEGETABLE SALAD

| | |
|---|---|
| 1 sm. carrot | 1/8 head of cabbage |
| ¼ of a green pepper | 3 radishes |
| 1 sm. white turnip | 1 sm. onion |
| 1 stalk celery | Lettuce |

Grate all vegetables together. Serve on lettuce leaf with salad dressing.

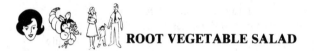

## ROOT VEGETABLE SALAD

2 carrots        2 parsnips same size as carrots

Grate carrots and parsnips very fine. Add a little chopped onion. Moisten with preferred dressing and serve on lettuce leaves. Parsnips are surprisingly sweet and good if very finely grated.

## VEGETABLE MEDLEY

| | |
|---|---|
| 2 c. freshly shelled small peas | 1 c. celery, diced fine |
| 1 c. fresh green beans, french sliced lengthwise | 2-3 pimimento peppers, sliced (or 1-4 oz. jar) |
| 1 med. bell pepper with seeds, chopped | 1 tsp. mustard seed |
| 4 green onions, chopped | 1 T. celery seed |

Mix together thoroughly with following dressing:

## DRESSING

| | |
|---|---|
| ¼ c. fresh lemon juice | 1 tsp. kelp |
| 6 T. cold pressed oil | Vegetable seasoning |
| 1 T. apple cider vinegar | |

 ## VEGETABLE SALAD #1

2 c. cabbage, chopped
3 stalks celery, chopped

3 green onions, chopped
1 carrot, grated

Toss together and moisten with favorite dressing. Serve on lettuce. Garnish with carrot sticks and parsley.

 ## VEGETABLE SALAD #2

½ of a small, firm, white cabbage
1 onion

10 radishes
3 ripe tomatoes

Chop everything up fine. Toss lightly together, heap on a platter, pour lemon dressing over, and garnish with lettuce hearts, watercress, or grated carrot.

 ## VEGETABLE WURST

1 oz. sweet potato, carrot or
  parsnips, ground
1 beet or turnip, ground
½ oz. horseradish, ground
1 oz. celery, parsley, leek or
  onions, minced

½ tsp. caraway seed, ground
2 oz. pignolias, ground with
  1 tsp. olive oil
1 oz. walnuts or other nut-
  meants, ground

Mix all together. Form into rolls ½ inch thick and two inches long. Roll into wax paper, chill, then serve.

 ## WALDORF SALAD

3 organic apples with
  bright red skins
½ c. celery
½ c. nut meats

Lemon juice or orange or
  nut cream
Red grapes

Chop up your apples, celery and nut meats. Add a little lemon juice or orange juice or nut cream to keep the apples from turning brown. Season to taste with a little mayonaise or your favorite dressing.

Serve in lettuce cups. Garnish with halves of red grapes.

 **WATERCRESS SALAD**

2 bunches of watercress      1 onion
½ sm. white cabbage      1 stalk of celery
1 green sweet pepper

Chop everything up fine with the watercress. Serve the chopped vegetables in a border of watercress. Serve with lemon juice and olive oil. Note: The combined flavor of cabbage and watercress is delicious.

 **WATERCRESS SALAD #2**

1 bunch watercress,      ½ tsp. Dijon mustard
    trimmed and washed      2½ T. lemon juice
¼ c. baco bits

Mix mustard and lemon juice well. Toss chilled watercress with the dressing and scatter with baco bits.

 **WATERCRESS AND
CELERY SALAD**

1 c. chopped watercress      Seed sauce
1 c. chopped tender celery stalks      Lettuce

Mix watercress and celery together with enough seed sauce to moisten. Serve on a freshly washed, crisp lettuce leaf. Garnish with parsley.

 **WINTER SALAD**

1 oz. carrot, grated      1 oz. nut meats, chopped
1 oz. celery, chopped fine      ½ oz. olive oil, (1 tsp.)
1/8 oz. horseradish, grated

Mix well and serve.

# DRESSINGS SAUCES RELISHES dIPS

**CHAPTER VIII.**

## AVOCADO DRESSING

| | |
|---|---|
| 2 avocados, mashed | 1 T. Vegetable seasoning |
| ½ c. finely chopped onions | ¼ c. lemon juice |
| 1 T. Kelp | |

Thin with Rejuvelac to desired consistency.

## SPECIAL AVOCADO MAYONNAISE

A GOLDEN SALAD DRESSING that is uncooked, and contains no salt, sugar, flour, eggs, cornstarch or other refined fillers. Contains only wholesome, natural ingredients.

| | |
|---|---|
| 6 oz. fresh pineapple juice | 1 T. vegetable salad oil, cold |
| 32 pecans or equal amount | pressed (sesame, soy, |
| other nuts | safflower) |
| 1 T. honey (optional) | ½ to a whole avocado |

Place the first four ingredients in the Liquidifer or Blender. Blend about two minutes until nuts are well liquified. If you don't have a blender, use nut butter instead of nuts and blend in a bowl.

Add the avocado and blend for about one minute, or until the dressing is emulsified. If you don't have a blender, mash the avocado with a fork and add to nut butter mixture.

This simple dressing is less rich in fats and sugars.

Variations: Use carrot juice or tomato juice. A bit of onion always perks up flavor.

## AVOCADO SAUCE

from Raychel Solomon, Hippocrates Health Institute, Lemon Grove, CA.

6 ripe tomatoes
3 sm. avocados (or 2 med.)
Dill weed
Oregano
Rejuvelac

½ yellow onion
1 clove garlic
Dr. Bronner's liquid
  bouillon to taste

Place above ingredients in a blender in the following order; Rejuvelac, tomatoes, Dr. Bronner's bouillon, avocado. Blend. Then add chopped garlic, onion and spices and blend very well. Serve over sprouts, greens and vegies.

## AVOCADO/ZUCCHINI SAUCE

Avocado
Zucchini
Rejuvelac

Lemon juice
Garlic
Veg. powdered seasoning

Blend all together well.

## BASIC SALAD DRESSING

¼ c. fresh lemon juice
6 T. oil (cold pressed)
1 T. kelp

1 T. Veg. seasoning
1 T. cider vinegar

Mix together in a salad dressing jar.

Take a risk and experiment as this is the only way to feel comfortable with these sauces!

## ANN WIGMORE'S BASIC SEED/NUT SAUCE

**2 c. seeds or nuts, (one at a time)        2 c. Rejuvelac or water**

If unfamiliar with these sauces, start with ½ cup seeds and ½ cup Rejuvelac or water. Grind seeds (sunflower, sesame, almonds, etc.) to meal with either an electric nut grinder or a hand mill. Blend in a blender with Rejuvelac or water until creamy consistency, approximately like a milkshake. Allow to stand at room temperature (68 - 75 degrees) until fermented:

with Rejuvelac, about 7-10 hours.

with water, about 15-50 hours.

temperature of the room is important.

Problems:

(1)    too thick (after fermented) — stir in Rejuvelac or water.

(2)    too thin (after fermented) — grind up seeds/nuts into meal and add.

(3)    too sour (overfermented) — tamari will take away sour taste if one must serve the sauce.

Variations:

— Combine 2 different seeds such as sunflower meal and almond meal, sesame and sunflower, etc.

— Make a delicious cheese by grinding very finely, 2 cups sunflower meal plus 1 cup almond meal, flavoring with chercil, dill, onion, tamari (a bit), parsley, radish, green pepper, kelp (lots).

Cheeses may be used to stuff celery sticks, green pepper sticks, tomatoes.

 ## BEET GARNISH

**Raw beets (sweet)                    Honey**
**Lemon juice**

Finely grate fresh sweet beets; add lemon juice and honey. Store in a glass jar and use just a little as a color garnish for other vegetable salads occasionally. The flavor is rather strong, so use sparingly unless you are very fond of it.

### BEET RELISH
from Geneviere Melton

| | |
|---|---|
| **1 grated beet** | **2 T. lemon juice** |
| **2 T. safflower oil** | |

Top grated salads or any salad with this. It aids digestion and assimilation and elimination. Keeps well in refrigerator a few days.

### BEET SAUCE

| | |
|---|---|
| **Raw beets** | **Lemon juice** |
| **Yellow squash** | **Garlic** |
| **Rejuvelac** | **Veg. seasoning or powdered** |

Blend all ingredients well.

### BLUEBERRY JELLY

| | |
|---|---|
| **Blueberries (fresh)** | **1 T. honey** |

Wash berries, drain thoroughly, place in blender with a teaspoon of honey; run till smooth, strain, pour into glass molds and set in refrigerator. This needs only its own selfcontained juices. It will jell in a little while. (Fresh berries must be used, the frozen ones do not jell so well).

Variation: Black raspberries tend to jell also, but will not usually become as stiff as the blueberries.

### CARROT SAUCE

| | |
|---|---|
| **Raw carrots** | **Raw coconut** |
| **Almonds** | |

Finely grate the carrots. Make a sauce with 1 part carrot, to one part almonds or coconut. Blend until smooth. Pour over grated carrots.

 **CAULIFLOWER SAUCE**

(for use on greens or sprouts) recommended by Joann Magram
of the San Diego Hippocrates Health Institute

| | |
|---|---|
| 1 head cauliflower, chopped | 2 T. onion, chopped |
| 1 green pepper | 1 lime |
| 1 clove garlic | 1 c. Rejuvelac |

In a blender, put most of the cauliflower. Mix in Rejuvelac. Blend. Add diced green pepper. Squeeze in juice of 1 lime. Blend well. Add finely chopped garlic and onion. Blend till smooth. Put in rest of cauliflower (small pieces). Serve over vegetables and/or greens.

 **CORN DRESSING**

| | |
|---|---|
| Fresh juicy sweet corn | Almond butter or sesame or sunflower butter |

Cut the corn from the cob. Juice the corn. To the juice thus obtained, add an equal amount of nut cream made from thoroughly mixing almond butter with water to the consistency of cream; add kelp to taste.

 **CORN RELISH**

| | |
|---|---|
| 1 c. fresh corn cut from cob | 1 tsp. celery seed |
| 1 c. cabbage, chopped | Kelp |
| 1 bell pepper, chopped | Vegetable seasoning |
| 1 sweet red pepper, chopped | ¼ to ½ c. fresh lemon juice |
| ½ c. celery, diced | ½ to 1 T. apple cider vinegar |

Toss together and serve, or may be used to stuff peppers.

## CUCUMBER SALAD DRESSING

**1 c. eggless mayonnaise**          **½ c. cucumber**
**Pinch of dill**

Blend in blender until smooth. Good on tossed salad.

## FRENCH DRESSING

**½ c. lemon juice**          **1 tomato**
**1 clove garlic**           **1 tsp. kelp**
**1 T. vegetable seasoning**

Blend together well in blender.

## FRESH GRAPE PUREE

**Fresh grapes**

Needs no other juice or water. Wash grapes, drain thoroughly. Place in blender; run till smooth. Strain, pour into glass molds and set in refrigerator. Do not blend too long as it may become too gritty with seed particles; strain through a ricer and serve in glass cups with a spoon as it is rich and thick. Use soon after preparing.

## GARLIC HERB DRESSING

Use the same basic recipe as in the Lemon Herb Dressing, eliminating the lemon juice, add ⅔ c. apple cider vinegar, ¼ tsp. dry mustard, and 1 clove garlic, peeled and split. After the flavors are blended, the garlic may be discarded (a day or two later).

## GREEN CHILI RELISH

3 green chili peppers, rinse and
    remove seeds and membrane
3 peeled tomatoes or 1½ c.
    tomatoes, strained. For milder
    relish add more tomato

2 small green onions
1 tsp. apple cider vinegar
1 clove minced garlic
Kelp to taste

Chop chile peppers, tomatos and onions. Add rest of ingredients and mix thoroughly.

## GREEN TOMATILLO TACO SAUCE

1 c. finely chopped tomatillos
    (Mexican tart green tomatoes)
½ c. finely chopped onion or
    5-6 green onions, chopped

2-3 chopped hot chili peppers
1 T. kelp
Pinch of fresh chopped
    coriandrum (Chinese parsley
    or Mexican cilatro)

Mix all together and refrigerate at least 2 hours. Makes 1½ cups.

## GREEN SALAD DRESSING

2 c. spinach (or indoor greens
    from sprouts growing one
    week in light)
1 c. water
½ avocado

4 T. sunflower seed meal
    (finely ground sunflower
    seeds)
1 T. kelp
Vegetable seasoning to taste

Put water in blender, drop in other ingredients, blending to desired consistency.

 **GUACAMOLE #1**

Avocado                     Kelp
Tomato                      Garlic
Red bell pepper

Blend until smooth

 **GUACAMOLE #2**

Avocado                     Vegetable seasoning
Kelp

Blend until smooth.

 **GUACAMOLE #3**

Avocado                     Lemon juice
Kelp                        Chopped onion
Vegetable seasoning         Garlic

Blend until smooth.

 **GUACAMOLE DIP #4**

2 or 3 ripe avocadoes       ½ onion, chopped fine
1 tomato, chopped & mashed  Hot peppers, chopped fine
1 T. kelp                   2 tsp. veg. seasoning

Mash avocadoes, stir in rest of ingredients to taste.
This may be thinned a little with rejuvelac to make a salad dressing.

## GUACAMOLE

from Raychel Solomon, Hippocrates Health Institute, Lemon Grove, CA.

| | |
|---|---|
| 3 medium avocados | 3 tomatoes, diced |
| 1 yellow onion, chopped fine | 1 lemon, juiced |
| 1 T. oregano | 1 tsp. dill weed |
| Dr. Bronner's bouillon to taste | 1 clove garlic (optional) |

Mix avocado and onion lightly. Add in oregano, juice of lemon, dill weed, and garlic. Add Dr. Bronner's bouillon liquid to taste. Stir well. Spread tomatoes on top of mixture and refrigerate (this prevents coloring of avocado). Mix just before serving.

## HERB DRESSING

| | |
|---|---|
| ½ tsp. thyme (ground) | ½ c. cold pressed oil |
| ¼ tsp. marjoram (ground) | 3 T. apple cider vinegar |
| ¼ tsp. tarragon (ground) | 1 T. fresh parsley, chopped fine |
| ½ tsp. basil (ground) | ½ tsp. sea salt (or 1 tsp kelp) |

Shake vigorously in covered jar till blended. Allow to stand in refrigerator til flavors are blended.

*Garnishes add to the salad's interest.* For vegetable or main-dish salads, use pimiento and green or red pepper strips, radishes, watercress, parsley or mint sprigs, carrot or celery curls, twisted lemon slices, chives or other fresh herbs.

## HORSERADISH AND
## FERMENTED BEET JUICE DIP

| | |
|---|---|
| Horseradish root | Kelp |
| Fermented beet juice | Vegetable seasoning |

Peel horseradish and grate fine. Add just enough fermented beet juice to moisten and season with kelp and vegetable seasoning.

## HOT SAUCE

2 c. chopped tomatoes
1 stalk celery, diced
1 onion, diced
1 green pepper, diced

Kelp
1 T. cider vinegar
1 T. honey
1 hot green or yellow chili,
    peeled & diced (or 2)

Combine tomatoes. celery, onion, green pepper, kelp, vinegar, honey and chili. Blend well. Cover tightly and chill overnight to blend flavors.

## HUMUS

3 c. sprouted garbanzo beans
1 clove garlic, minced
1 T. cider vinegar
3 T. olive oil

1 tsp. kelp
1/8 tsp. cayenne
Paprika

Blend beans with garlic until smooth, then gradually add vinegar, oil, kelp, cayenne. Place in a bowl and sprinkle with paprika. Flavor is improved if it stands for 2 hours. Can be served at room temperature or chilled. Use raw vegetables to dip. Beans may be put through food grinder before blending for a smoother texture.

## ITALIAN GREEN SAUCE

½ c. minced parsley
¼ c. chopped pignola nuts
2 T. drained capers, chopped, or
1 T. green nasturtium seeds
¼ c. ground sunflower seeds

6 pitted black olives, minced
3 T. apple cider vinegar
Kelp
1 tsp. fresh chili pepper
1 tsp. minced chives, onion or
    garlic

Mix together thoroughly and serve.

## IMPROVED MAYONNAISE

½ oz. pignolas, ground               1 oz. lemon juice
   (pine nuts)
   Mix two together and let stand 15 minutes.
½ oz. olive oil

Add oil and beat into a cream. The flavor may be varied to suit by adding half tsp. of either ground caraway seed, or mustard seed.

## TAHINI MAYONNAISE

1 c. Tahini (Sesame Nut Butter        ½ c. lemon juice
   which can be bought in a            1 c. water
   Health Food Store, but it's         Vegetable seasoning
   better made fresh)                  Garlic powder

Blend to make a smooth dressing.

## LEMON HERB DRESSING

1 stalk celery & leaves               2 sprigs parsley
1 sm. green onion & tops,             ¼ tsp. dried sweet basil
   chopped very fine                  ⅔ c. cold pressed salad oil
1 tsp. veg. broth & seasoning         $1/16$ tsp. marjoram
½ tsp. sea salt (or 1 tsp. kelp)      Juice of one lemon

Shake vigorously in covered jar til blended. Allow to stand in refrigerator till flavors are blended.

## MOLE' SAUCE

| | |
|---|---|
| 1 medium chili | 1 T. almonds |
| 2 tortillas, shredded | 1 T. sesame seed |
| 2 red tomatoes | 2 cloves garlic |
| 2 green tomatoes | 2 oz. carob powder |
| 1 T. pumpkin seeds | |

Grind all together to make an interesting different sauce.

## NUT OR SEED BUTTER DRESSING

1 part lemon juice                2 parts nut or seed butter

Mix well together.

## NUT CREAM DRESSING

1 c. almond butter                2 T. water or lemon juice

Blend together in a small bowl with a spoon.

Or:

Natural nut meats                Water or lemon juice

Blend in your blender by adding nut meats to the liquid and blend until smooth and the consistency you want.

## ONION DRESSING

| | |
|---|---|
| ½ c. safflower oil | ½ tsp. kelp |
| 1 lemon | 1 large onion |

Add the juice of the lemon to the oil and kelp and beat well. Add the juice of the onion and mix well.

# ONION RELISH

| | |
|---|---|
| **Onions** | **Honey** |
| **1 lemon** | **Jar** |

Slice onions thinly into jar; add the juice of 1 lemon to a pint, then add a tablespoon of honey; tamp down firmly in jar. This keeps almost indefinitely.

# PARSLEY DRESSING

| | |
|---|---|
| **½ c. safflower oil** | **½ tsp. kelp** |
| **1 lemon** | **1 bunch parsley** |

Add the juice of the lemon to the oil and kelp and beat well. Add the juice of the parsley and mix well.

# PARSLEY SAUCE

| | |
|---|---|
| **1 c. parsley, finely chopped** | **Juice of ½ lemon** |
| **1 c. green onions, finely chopped** | **Kelp** |
| **1 clove garlic, pressed** | |

Add water or Rejuvelac to desired consistency. Serve over grated or sliced raw potatoes, or as a dressing for salads.

# PINEAPPLE AVOCADO DRESSING

| | |
|---|---|
| **1 c. fresh pineapple juice** | **6 almonds** |
| **1 avocado** | |

Blend until smooth in blender the almonds and the juice, then add the avocado and blend lightly.

## RED SALSA TACO SAUCE

2 c. fresh tomatoes, blended
1 can (small) peeled green ortegas
   or 2 fresh, minced, & seeded
1 sweet onion, chopped fine
1 T. kelp

2 cloves garlic, crushed
   through garlic press
Juice of 2 lemons
1 very ripe avocado, diced
   finely

## SALAD DRESSING

¼ c. olive oil
¼ c. cold pressed safflower oil

3 T. lemon juice (fresh)
3 T. apple cider vinegar

Mix all together and chill.

## SALSA
(Chilled Mexican Sauce)

2 c. fresh tomatoes
1 can (small) peeled green
   ortegas minced, or fresh
   jalapino peppers may be used
1 sweet onion

2 cloves garlic, crushed
   through a press
Juice of 2 lemons
1 very ripe avocado
1 tsp. kelp

Cut up everything and blend on slow speed. Do not liquefy. Refrigerate.

## SESAME DRESSING

2 T. sesame seeds, ground
1 T. lemon juice
1 tsp. safflower oil

1 T. vegetable seasoning
Optional - a pinch of chili
   powder

Blend well, Refrigerate.

 **SESAME CREAM DRESSING**

Sesame butter (Tahini in Health          2 T. water or lemon juice
Food Stores

Blend to gether in a small bowl with a spoon to desired consistency.
Variation: Use sunflower seed butter or pumpkin seed butter.

 **SIMPLE SAUCE**

1 c. seed sauce                          4 T. minced parsley
4 T. lemon juice                         ½ c. finely chopped cucumber
2 T. minced onion                        1 sm. clove garlic (run through
                                              press)

Mix altogether. Use as salad dressing.

**SUNFLOWER SAUCE**

2 c. sunflower seeds                     ¼ tsp. dried parsley
½ c. lemon juice                         1 tsp. kelp
¼ tsp. sage                              1 tsp. vegetable seasoning
¼ tsp. basil                             Rejuvelac
¼ tsp. savory

Blend in blender with enough Rejuvelac to give desired consistency.
This may be left at room temperature for a fermented sauce.

**FERMENTED SUNFLOWER & SESAME SAUCES**
from Raychel Solomon, Hippocrates Health Institute

Sunflower seeds (hulled) or              Rejuvelac
Sesame Seeds (unhulled)

Grind one of the above seeds to a fine powder, add Rejuvelac (about ⅓ cup Rejuvelac to 1 cup of seeds) place in incubator for 4 to 6 hours or in the sun for 8 hours. When in the incubator put a plate over the bowl. The longer it ferments the stronger and more enzymatic. Refrigerate; add more Rejuvelac to the consistency desired. Keeps for several days under refrigeration.

## SUPAWN

2 oz. green corn pulp (young)
   sweet corn or white corn cut
   off the cob)

1 oz. almonds or pignolas -
   or substitute sunflower seeds
½ oz. celery

Put all through a meat grinder together. Serve as a pudding or sauce.

## FRESH TOMATILLO SAUCE
### (Mexican tart green tomatoes)

1 c. finely chopped tomatillos
½ c. finely chopped onion
2-3 tsp. chopped hot chilis

¼ c. lightly packed Chinese
   parsley (cilantro)
Kelp

Mix all together. Chill up to 2 hours. Makes 1½ cups.

## TOMATO AVOCADO DRESSING

1 large ripe avocado
1 med. size tomato, chopped
2 green onions, chopped fine
3 T. lemon juice

1 T. olive oil
½ tsp. vegetable seasoning
1 T. lecithin granules
Cayenne pepper to taste

Blend all together until smooth. Lemon juice will protect the color of the avocado.

## TOMATO LEMON SAUCE

4 tomatoes
Juice of one small lemon

1 T. ground wheat sprouts
½ tsp. thyme & marjoram
    combined

Blend well.

## TOMATO SAUCE

Tomatoes
Rejuvelac
Lime juice

Garlic
Olive oil
Veg. powdered seasoning

Blend all together well.

## VARIETY SAUCE

6-8 ripe tomatoes
1-2 cloves garlic
¼ c. lemon juice

1 bunch green onions, chopped
1 T. kelp

Peel and chop the tomatoes, add chopped onion, garlic and seasoning. This is good on sandwiches or salads.

## VEGETABLE PUDDING OR RELISH

1 oz. carrot, ground
1 oz. cabbage, ground

½ oz. horseradish, grated (tsp.)
1 oz. pignolias, ground
    with 1 tsp. olive oil

Mix together and serve by the spoonful.

## VEGETABLE SAUCES
from Raychel Solomon, Hippocrates Health Institute, Lemon Grove, CA.

| | |
|---|---|
| **2-3 carrots** | **1 tsp. Dr. Bronner's** |
| **1 zucchini or beets** | **Garlic to taste** |
| **3 small tomatoes** | **Basil to taste** |
| **2-3 celery stalks** | **Oregano to taste** |
| **3-4 sprigs parsley** | **Cumin to taste** |
| **1 onion** | **A little avocado emulsifies mixture** |

First pulverize the carrots, chop the zucchini, onion, celery, and tomatoes. Blend the above ingredients with Rejuvelac. Usually served in the evening because it's lighter.

## SEED BUTTER
from Dale Gardner

**Sesame Seed**          **Sunflower Seed**
**Rejuvelac**

Grind in Molinex grinder (nut and coffee grinder) 1 part sesame seed and 3 parts sunflower seed. Put in a blender with equal parts of Rejuvelac or water and blend until smooth. May be seasoned with garlic, onions, etc., if desired.

## *SOME LETTERS FROM LIVE FOODS FANS*

We started the Live Food diet eight weeks ago. My husband has lost weight - twenty pounds (needed as he was on a restricted diet because of three heart attacks three years ago and wasn't losing). He says it's so great to eat and feel full. I am getting my strength back and never felt better. I had high blood pressure and two pills a day made me feel terrible and my blood pressure stayed up around 150/100. I have now stopped the pills (the day we started the Live Food diet). My blood pressure is down to 130/100 and no doubt will go down to 120/100 as the doctor would like to see it.

M. & B. V., Fall City, WA

# SPROUTING

## Did YOU know?

**CHAPTER IX.**

## CHAPTER IX.
# DID YOU KNOW?

There is a vegetable that will grow in any climate, rival meat in nutritional value, grow to maturity in 3-5 days, and can be eaten without preparation. In addition it should require no soil or sunshine, could be planted any time of the year, rivals tomatoes in vitamin C, and has no waste.[1]

The food is sprouts.*

You can convert one pound of seed into ten pounds of food in 3 to 6 days; and the stored seed keeps for years.[2]

Buy seeds and beans and grains from Health Food Stores so they will be untreated with chemicals, thus able to support life. Fumigated seeds and beans will sour instead of sprouting. One cannot help wondering if these seeds, beans and grains that have been fumigated do more harm than good to our bodies. As for me, I no longer take the chance.

Soak small seeds like alfalfa 4 hours; large seeds and beans, 15 hrs. at room temperature. Drain thoroughly.

JAR METHOD — For small seeds, rotate the jar so seeds will stick to the sides. Lay on side in cabinet. Rinse twice a day, draining thoroughly. Use a wide mouth jar. Cover end with lid from sprouting kit bought in Health Food Store, cheesecloth, nylon net, or nylon stocking, securing with string or rubber band.

1. McCoy, Dr. Clive, Cornell University, in book by Oliver, M.H., *Add A Few Sprouts,* 1975, Keats Publishing, Inc. (36 Grove St., New Canaan, Conn.)

2. Ann Wigmore, D.D., N.D., PH.D., Hippocrates Health Institute, 25 Exeter Street, Boston, Mass. 02216.

* See *How I Conquered Cancer Naturally* by Eydie Mae with Chris Loeffler for "Why" you should sprout, and more detailed instructions on sprouting. This book is available for $2.95 from Production House, 4307 Euclid Avenue, San Diego, CA. 92115, or for $3.95 from Harvest House, 17845 Sky Park Circle, Irvine, CA. 92714.

PRESSURE SPROUTING — Use for sweet, small sprouts of mung beans. Buy three plastic containers — size according to your use. I use 1½ qt. size freezer containers. Punch holes in the bottom of one with an ice pick. Stack this one inside a second container. Put mung beans inside the container with the holes. Cover with water and let set 15 hrs. Remove the container with the beans and allow to drain. Then stack it inside the third container. The water left from soaking the mung beans may be poured over your plants and fresh water put in this second container. Set the second container filled with water about half full on top of the beans, putting pressure on the beans. Rinse and alternate cartons twice a day. In three days, the sprouts should be the size of the bean and ready for use. A french fry basket makes a good "shaker" to remove the hard unsprouted beans.

**ALFALFA** — 2 T. will fill a 2 qt. jar
Room temperature — Soak 4 hrs.
Rinse twice a day
Length — about 2 inches
3-5 days

**MUNG** — 1 cup = approx. 4 cups sprouts (jar method)
Room temperature — Soak 15 hrs.
Rinse twice a day
Length — about 2 inches
4 days

**GARBANZO** — 1 cup = 4 cups sprouts (jar method)
40 degrees — they like it cool to sprout
Soak 15 hrs.
Rinse once or twice a day
Length of bean
3-5 days

**LENTILS** — 1 cup = 6 cups sprouts (jar method)
Room temperature — Soak 12-15 hrs.
Rinse twice a day
1 inch
3-4 days

**RADISH** —     1 T. = approx. 1½ cups
Room temperature — Soak 4 hrs.
Rinse twice a day
Length 1 inch
3-5 days
Use sparingly as they are "radish hot".

**WHEAT** —     1 cup = 4 cups sprouts
Room temperature — Soak 15 hrs.
Length of grain
3-4 days

**BROWN RICE -** 1 cup = 2 - 2½ cups
Room temperature — Soak 15 hrs.
Rinse two or three times a day
Length of grain
3-5 days
Rice contains all of the essential amino acids.

## SOUR LENTIL SPROUTS

**1½ oz. lentils**                    **1½ oz. lemon juice**

Soak overnight in lemon juice till soft. Pour lemon juice off into pitcher. Cover juice and put in refrigerator. Sprout lentils continuing to use same lemon juice to rinse lentils for 3 days. Use sour lentil sprouts in salads . . . mix with nuts and sunflower seeds for a party mix.

## SPROUTED BEANS

**Dried pinto beans or**
**Dried kidney beans or**
**Dried lima beans etc.**

Soak for 15 hrs. Sprout for 3 days before cooking. Use low heat — under 120 degrees — for 4 to 5 hours or until tender.

Sprouting increases the nutritional value and also activates the enzymes which in turn helps to eliminate the flatulance that usually goes along with beans.

Seeds, nuts, and beans increase in vitamin and nutritional value after sprouting, sometimes with a very high percentage.

Any mixture of sprouts may be tossed together with other vegetables, or eaten alone with or without dressing or added to a green, tossed salad.

Alfalfa may be used in place of lettuce.

Sprouts can be put through your own juicer to drink, or put in separate bowls for each to choose their own.

Top with a fermented sauce or you favorite salad dressing.

## HOW TO GROW INDOOR GREENS

### BUCKWHEAT LETTUCE

**Organically grown buckwheat seeds**

Soak the seeds and plant the same as you do wheat grass. Harvest when 3-4 inches.

### SUNFLOWER LETTUCE SPROUTS

**Unhulled sunflower seeds (Use birdseed — this hasn't been treated)**

Soak the seeds and plant the same as you do wheat grass. Harvest when 3-4 inches.

Soak small seeds 4 hours.
Soak large seeds 15 hours.

### For Incubation —

I use a one hundred watt light bulb in the oven in place of the oven bulb. You can build one from a crate or whatever and use the correct size bulb to maintain a temperature under 120 degrees F. Maybe even a corner of the kitchen cabinet that you never use much could be utilized in this way.

# DID YOU KNOW?
## COMPOSITION OF FOODS, 100 GRAMS, EDIBLE PORTIONS, 3½ oz.

| | PROTEIN | FAT | CARBOHYDRATE | CALCIUM | PHOSPHORUS | IRON | SODIUM | POTASSIUM | VITAMIN A | THIAMINE B-1 | RIBOFLAVIN B-2 | NIACIN | ASCORBIC ACID-C |
|---|---|---|---|---|---|---|---|---|---|---|---|---|---|
| | Grams | Grams | Grams | Mg | Mg | Mg | Mg | Mg | Mg I.U. | I.U. | Mg | Mg | Mg |
| Almonds | 18.6 | 54.2 | 19.5 | 234 | 504 | 4.7 | 4 | 773 | 0 | .24 | .92 | 3.5 | Trace |
| Apples | .2 | .6 | 14.5 | 7 | 10 | .3 | 1 | 110 | 90 | .03 | .02 | .1 | 4 |
| Apricots | 1.0 | .2 | 12.8 | 17 | 23 | .5 | 1 | 281 | 2700 | .03 | .04 | .6 | 10 |
| Artichokes | 2.0 | .2 | 10.6 | 51 | 88 | 1.3 | 43 | 430 | 160 | .08 | .05 | 1.0 | 12 |
| Asparagus | 2.5 | .2 | 5.0 | 22 | 62 | 1.0 | 2 | 278 | 900 | .18 | .20 | 1.5 | 33 |
| Avocados | 2.1 | 16.4 | 6.3 | 10 | 42 | .6 | 4 | 604 | 290 | .11 | .20 | 1.6 | 14 |
| Bananas | 1.1 | .2 | 22.2 | 8 | 26 | .7 | 1 | 370 | 190 | .05 | .06 | .7 | 10 |
| Barley | 8.2 | 1.0 | 78.8 | 16 | 189 | 2.0 | 3 | 160 | 0 | .12 | .05 | 3.1 | 0 |
| Beans (White) | 22.3 | 1.6 | 61.3 | 144 | 425 | 7.8 | 19 | 1196 | 0 | .65 | .22 | 2.4 | — |
| Beans (Pinto) | 22.9 | 1.2 | 63.7 | 135 | 457 | 6.4 | 10 | 984 | — | .84 | .21 | 2.2 | — |
| Beans (Lima) | 8.4 | .5 | 22.1 | 52 | 142 | 2.8 | 2 | 650 | 290 | .24 | .12 | 1.4 | 29 |
| Beans (Mung) | 24.2 | 1.3 | 60.3 | 118 | 340 | 7.7 | 6 | 1028 | 80 | .38 | .21 | 2.6 | — |
| Beans (Snap) | 1.9 | .2 | 7.1 | 56 | 44 | .8 | 7 | 243 | 600 | .08 | .11 | .5 | 19 |
| Beans (Mung sprouts) | 3.8 | .2 | 6.6 | 19 | 64 | 1.3 | 5 | 223 | 20 | .13 | .13 | .8 | 19 |
| Beet (Red) | 1.6 | .1 | 9.9 | 16 | 33 | .7 | 60 | 335 | 20 | .03 | .05 | .4 | 10 |
| Beet (Greens) | 2.2 | .3 | 4.6 | 119 | 40 | 3.3 | 130 | 570 | 6100 | .10 | .22 | .4 | 30 |
| Blackberries | 1.2 | .9 | 12.9 | 32 | 19 | .9 | 1 | 170 | 200 | .03 | .04 | .4 | 21 |
| Blueberries | .7 | .5 | 15.3 | 15 | 13 | 1.0 | 1 | 81 | 100 | .03 | .06 | .5 | 14 |
| Breadfruit | 1.7 | .3 | 26.2 | 33 | 32 | 1.2 | 15 | 439 | 40 | .11 | .03 | .9 | 29 |
| Cabbage | 1.3 | .2 | 5.4 | 49 | 29 | .4 | 20 | 233 | 130 | .05 | .05 | .3 | 47 |
| Carrots | 1.1 | .2 | 9.7 | 37 | 36 | .7 | 47 | 341 | 11000 | .06 | .05 | .6 | 8 |

| | Grams | Grams | Grams | Mg. | Mg. | Mg. | Mg. | Mg. | Mg. | I.U. | Mg. | Mg. | Mg. |
|---|---|---|---|---|---|---|---|---|---|---|---|---|---|
| Cauliflower | 2.7 | .2 | 5.2 | 25 | 56 | 1.1 | 13 | 295 | 60 | .11 | .10 | .7 | 78 |
| Celery | .9 | .1 | 3.9 | 39 | 28 | .3 | 126 | 341 | 240 | .03 | .03 | .3 | 9 |
| Chard (Swiss) | 2.4 | .3 | 4.6 | 88 | 39 | 3.2 | 147 | 550 | 6500 | .06 | .17 | .5 | 32 |
| Cherries (Sweet) | 1.3 | .3 | 17.4 | 22 | 19 | .4 | 2 | 191 | 110 | .05 | .06 | .4 | 10 |
| Chives | 1.8 | .3 | 5.8 | 69 | 44 | 1.7 | — | 250 | 5800 | .08 | .13 | .5 | 56 |
| Collards | 4.8 | .8 | 7.5 | 250 | 82 | 1.5 | — | 450 | 9300 | .16 | .31 | 1.7 | 152 |
| Corn (Field) | 8.9 | 3.9 | 72.2 | 22 | 268 | 2.1 | 1 | 284 | 490 | .37 | .12 | 2.2 | 0 |
| Corn (Sweet) | 3.5 | 1 | 22.1 | 3 | 111 | .7 | Trace | 280 | 400 | .15 | .12 | 1.7 | 12 |
| Cowpeas (Garbanzo) | 9.0 | .8 | 21.8 | 27 | 172 | 2.3 | 2 | 541 | 370 | .43 | .13 | 1.6 | 29 |
| Crabapples | .4 | .3 | 17.8 | 6 | 13 | .3 | 1 | 110 | 40 | .03 | .02 | .1 | 8 |
| Eggplant | 1.2 | .2 | 5.6 | 12 | 26 | .7 | 2 | 214 | 10 | .05 | .05 | .6 | 5 |
| Elderberries | 2.6 | .5 | 16.4 | 38 | 28 | 1.6 | — | 300 | 600 | .07 | .06 | .5 | 36 |
| Endive | 1.7 | .1 | 4.1 | 81 | 54 | 1.7 | 14 | 294 | 3300 | .07 | .14 | .5 | 10 |
| Figs | 1.2 | .3 | 20.3 | 35 | 22 | .6 | 2 | 194 | 80 | .06 | .05 | .4 | 2 |
| Garlic | 6.2 | .2 | 30.8 | 29 | 202 | 1.5 | 19 | 529 | Trace | .25 | .08 | .5 | 15 |
| Gooseberries | .8 | .2 | 9.7 | 18 | 15 | .5 | 1 | 155 | 290 | — | — | — | 33 |
| Grapefruit | .5 | .1 | 10.6 | 16 | 16 | .4 | 1 | 135 | 80 | .04 | .02 | .2 | 38 |
| Grapes | 1.3 | 1 | 15.7 | 16 | 12 | .4 | 3 | 158 | 100 | .05 | .03 | .3 | 4 |
| Guavas | .8 | .6 | 15.0 | 23 | 42 | .9 | 4 | 289 | 280 | .05 | .05 | 1.2 | 242 |
| Kale | 6.0 | .8 | 9 | 249 | 93 | 2.7 | 75 | 378 | 10000 | .16 | .26 | 2.1 | 186 |
| Kumquats | .9 | .1 | 17.1 | 63 | 23 | .4 | 7 | 236 | 600 | .08 | .10 | — | 36 |
| Leeks | 2.2 | .3 | 11.2 | 52 | 50 | 1.1 | 5 | 347 | 40 | .11 | .06 | .5 | 17 |
| Lemons | 1.1 | .3 | 8.2 | 26 | 16 | .6 | 2 | 138 | 20 | .04 | .02 | .1 | 53 |
| Lentils | 24.7 | 1.1 | 60.1 | 79 | 377 | 6.8 | 30 | 790 | 60 | .37 | .22 | 2 | — |
| Lettuce | 1.2 | .2 | 2.5 | 35 | 26 | 2.0 | 9 | 264 | 970 | .06 | .06 | .3 | 8 |
| Mushrooms | 2.7 | .3 | 4.4 | 6 | 116 | .8 | 15 | 414 | Trace | .10 | .46 | 4.2 | 3 |
| Mushmelons | .7 | .1 | 7.5 | 14 | 16 | .4 | 12 | 251 | 3400 | .04 | .03 | .6 | 33 |
| Mustard greens | 3.0 | .5 | 5.6 | 183 | 50 | 3.0 | 32 | 377 | 7000 | .11 | .22 | .8 | 97 |
| Nectarines | .6 | Trace | 17.1 | 4 | 24 | .5 | 6 | 294 | 1650 | — | — | — | 13 |
| Okra | 2.4 | .3 | 7.6 | 92 | 51 | .6 | 3 | 249 | 520 | .17 | .21 | 1.0 | 31 |
| Onions (Dry) | 1.5 | .1 | 8.7 | 27 | 36 | .5 | 10 | 157 | 40 | .03 | .04 | .2 | 10 |
| Onions (Green) | 1.5 | .2 | 8.2 | 51 | 39 | 1.0 | 5 | 231 | 2000 | .05 | .05 | .4 | 32 |

# DID YOU KNOW?

## COMPOSITION OF FOODS, 100 GRAMS, EDIBLE PORTIONS, 3½ oz.

| | PROTEIN | FAT | CARBOHYDRATE | CALCIUM | PHOSPHORUS | IRON | SODIUM | POTASSIUM | VITAMIN A | THIAMINE B-1 | RIBOFLAVIN B-2 | NIACIN | ASCORBIC ACID-C |
|---|---|---|---|---|---|---|---|---|---|---|---|---|---|
| | Grams | Grams | Grams | Mg. | Mg. | Mg. | Mg. | Mg. | Mg. | I.U. | Mg. | Mg. | Mg. |
| Oranges | 1.0 | .2 | 12.2 | 41 | 20 | .4 | 1 | 200 | 200 | .10 | .04 | .4 | 50 |
| Papayas | .6 | .1 | 10.0 | 20 | 16 | .3 | 3 | 234 | 1750 | .04 | .04 | .3 | 56 |
| Parsley | 3.6 | .6 | 8.5 | 203 | 63 | 6.2 | 45 | 727 | 8500 | .12 | .26 | 1.2 | 172 |
| Parsnips | 1.7 | .5 | 17.5 | 50 | 77 | .7 | 12 | 541 | 30 | .08 | .09 | .2 | 16 |
| Peaches | .6 | .1 | 9.7 | 9 | 19 | .5 | 1 | 202 | 1330 | .02 | .05 | 1.0 | 7 |
| Peanuts (Raw) | 26.0 | 47.5 | 18.6 | 69 | 401 | 2.1 | 5 | 674 | — | 1.14 | .13 | 17.2 | 0 |
| Pears | .7 | .4 | 15.3 | 8 | 11 | .3 | 2 | 130 | 20 | .02 | .04 | .1 | 4 |
| Peas (Edible pod) | 3.4 | .2 | 12.0 | 62 | 90 | .7 | — | 170 | 680 | .28 | .12 | — | 21 |
| Peas (Green) | 6.3 | .4 | 14.4 | 26 | 116 | 1.9 | 2 | 316 | 640 | .35 | .14 | 2.9 | 27 |
| Pecans | 9.2 | 71.2 | 14.6 | 73 | 289 | 2.4 | Trace | 603 | 130 | .86 | .13 | .9 | 2 |
| Peppers (Hot red) | 3.7 | 2.3 | 18.1 | 29 | 78 | 1.2 | — | — | 21600 | .22 | .36 | 4.4 | 369 |
| Peppers (Sweet green) | 1.2 | .2 | 4.8 | 9 | 22 | .7 | 13 | 213 | 420 | .08 | .08 | .5 | 128 |
| Persimmons | .7 | .4 | 19.7 | 6 | 26 | .3 | 6 | 174 | 2700 | .03 | .02 | .1 | 11 |
| Pickles (Cucumber) | .9 | .2 | 17.9 | 32 | 27 | 1.8 | 673 | — | 140 | Trace | .03 | Trace | 9 |
| Pineapple | .4 | .2 | 13.7 | 17 | 8 | .5 | 1 | 146 | 70 | .09 | .03 | .2 | 17 |
| Plums | .5 | Trace | 17.8 | 18 | 17 | .5 | 2 | 299 | 300 | .08 | .03 | .5 | — |
| Pomegranate | .5 | .3 | 16.4 | 3 | 8 | .3 | 3 | 259 | Trace | .03 | .03 | .3 | 4 |
| Potatoes | 2.1 | .1 | 17.1 | 7 | 53 | .6 | 3 | 407 | Trace | .10 | .04 | 1.5 | 20 |
| Rhubarb | .6 | .1 | 3.7 | 96 | 18 | .8 | 2 | 251 | 100 | .03 | .07 | .3 | 9 |
| Rice (Brown) | 7.5 | 1.9 | 77.4 | 32 | 221 | 1.6 | 9 | 214 | 0 | .34 | .05 | 4.7 | 0 |

| | Grams | Grams | Grams | Mg. | Mg. | Mg. | Mg. | Mg. | Mg. | I.U. | Mg. | Mg. | Mg. |
|---|---|---|---|---|---|---|---|---|---|---|---|---|---|
| Rye | 12.1 | 1.7 | 73.4 | 38 | 376 | 3.7 | 1 | 467 | 0 | .43 | .22 | 1.6 | 0 |
| Sapotes | 1.8 | .6 | 31.6 | 39 | 28 | 1.0 | — | — | 410 | .01 | .02 | 1.8 | 20 |
| Seaweed (Kelp) | — | 1.1 | — | 1093 | 240 | — | 3007 | 5273 | — | — | — | — | — |
| Seaweed (Dulce) | — | 3.2 | — | 296 | 267 | — | 2085 | 8060 | — | — | — | — | — |
| Sesame Seeds | 18.6 | 49.1 | 21.6 | 1160 | 616 | 10.5 | 60 | 725 | 30 | .98 | .24 | 5.4 | 0 |
| Soybeans | 10.9 | 5.1 | 13.2 | 67 | 225 | 2.8 | — | — | 690 | .44 | .16 | 1.4 | 29 |
| Spinach | 3.2 | .3 | 4.3 | 93 | 51 | 3.1 | 71 | 470 | 8100 | .10 | .20 | .6 | 51 |
| Squash | 1.1 | .1 | 4.2 | 28 | 29 | .4 | 1 | 202 | 410 | .05 | .09 | 1.0 | 22 |
| Strawberries | .7 | .5 | 8.4 | 21 | 21 | 1.0 | 1 | 164 | 60 | .03 | .07 | .6 | 59 |
| Sunflower Seeds | 24.0 | 47.3 | 19.9 | 120 | 837 | 7.1 | 30 | 920 | 50 | 1.96 | .23 | 5.4 | — |
| Sweet Potatoes | 1.7 | .4 | 26.3 | 32 | 47 | .7 | 10 | 243 | 8800 | .10 | .06 | .6 | 21 |
| Tangerines | .8 | .2 | 11.6 | 40 | 18 | .4 | 2 | 126 | 420 | .06 | .02 | .1 | 31 |
| Tomatoes | 1.1 | .2 | 4.7 | 13 | 27 | .5 | 3 | 244 | 900 | .06 | .04 | .7 | 23 |
| Turnips | 1.0 | .2 | 6.6 | 39 | 30 | .5 | 49 | 268 | Trace | .04 | .07 | .6 | 36 |
| Turnip (Greens) | 3.0 | .3 | 5.0 | 246 | 58 | 1.8 | — | — | 7600 | .21 | .39 | .8 | 139 |
| Vinegar (Apple cider) | Trace | 0 | 5.9 | 6 | 9 | .6 | 1 | 100 | — | — | — | — | — |
| Walnuts (English) | 14.8 | 64.0 | 15.8 | 99 | 380 | 3.1 | 2 | 450 | 30 | .33 | .13 | .9 | 2 |
| Watercress | 2.2 | .3 | 3.0 | 151 | 54 | 1.7 | 52 | 282 | 4900 | .08 | .16 | .9 | 79 |
| Watermelon | .5 | .2 | 6.4 | 7 | 10 | .5 | 1 | 100 | 590 | .03 | .03 | .2 | 7 |
| Wheat (Hard red winter) | 12.3 | 1.8 | 71.7 | 46 | 354 | 3.4 | 3 | 370 | 0 | .52 | .12 | 4.3 | 0 |
| Wheat (Soft spring white) | 9.4 | 2.0 | 75.4 | 36 | 394 | 3.0 | 3 | 390 | 0 | .53 | .12 | 5.3 | 0 |

**Composition of Foods Handbook #8. U.S. Dept. of Agriculture**

## *SOME LETTERS FROM LIVE FOODS FANS*

I just finished reading your book, "How I Conquered Cancer Naturally." I only wish I had read this book before I had a mastectomy. I had surgery..., a modified radical. The doctor said my tumor was so tiny they almost missed it and I had no node involvement. My family Doctor used to be a pathologist and I felt he might have researched other methods but when I was put in the hands of a surgeon the outcome was surgery. I guess I was just too scared of that word cancer.

The other morning on the Good Morning America Show, a man and wife medical team, the Doctors Miller, said that after thirty-two years of cancer research they feel the secret to cure of cancer will be the enzymes and our diet.

R. L., Irvine, CA

# Ann Wigmore's Complete Meal Salad

**CHAPTER X.**

## ANN WIGMORE'S ORGANIC COMPLETE
### SALAD - One portion
(Her answer to malnutrition, high cost and poor quality food)

| | |
|---|---|
| ¼ avocado | ½ c. leafy greens |
| 7 slices cucumber | (grown indoors) |
| 1 c. mung bean sprouts | ⅛ c. salad oil |
| ½ c. raw sliced summer squash | 2 slices tomato, or red pepper |
| 2 T. sunflower seeds | Small bits dulse or kelp |

Sunflower greens or buckwheat greens fill the bill well for the leafy greens, only ½ cup needed. (See instructions on growing indoor greens.) Start your mung bean sprouts several days ahead. (See instructions on pressure sprouting.) Soak your sunflower seeds in water for 4 hrs. to make them easier to digest and crunchy (optional). Add a little lemon juice to your oil if you desire.

Toss all together. Makes one meal.


## ANALYSIS OF DR. WIGMORE'S
## COMPLETE MEAL SALAD
### By Dr. Harvey C. Lisle*

The "Complete Meal Salad" contains 543 calories, full vitamin, mineral, and enzyme-packed calories.

It also contains full proteins in quantity and quality.

Table I reveals the individual items which contain all 8 of the essential amino acids.

Table II gives the necessary data from which the proteins and calories of Table III are calculated.

Total protein for this one meal is 15 grams.

---

\* Dr. Harvey C. Lisle is a Chemical Engineer with 15 years industrial experience in food testing laboratories, including both animal and human foods.

**Table I.** Based on 100 grams edible portions. Mg. stands for milligrams.

| | Isoleucine | Leucine | Lysine | Methionine | Phyenylanine | Tryptophane | Theonine | Valine |
|---|---|---|---|---|---|---|---|---|
| | Mg. | Mg. | Mg. | Mg. | Mg. | Mg. | Mg. | Mg. |
| Avocado | — | — | 120 | 19 | — | 23 | — | — |
| Cucumber | 9 | 13 | 13 | 3 | 7 | 2 | 8 | 10 |
| Mung Beans | 213 | 346 | 258 | 42 | 182 | 27 | 118 | 224 |
| Summer Squash | 19 | 27 | 23 | 8 | 16 | 5 | 14 | 22 |
| Greens | 161 | 165 | 147 | 29 | 108 | 26 | 106 | 129 |
| Sunflower Seeds* | 1320 | 1824 | 912 | 456 | 1272 | 360 | 936 | 1416 |

*Especially excellent in containing all 8 essential amino acids.

## TABLE II.

| | PERCENTAGE OF PROTEIN | CALORIES PER 100 GRAMS |
|---|---|---|
| Avocado | 2.1 | 245 |
| Cucumber | 0.6 | 12 |
| Mung Bean Sprouts | 3.8 | 23 |
| Summer Squash | 0.6 | 16 |
| Leafy Greens | 2.3 | 20 |
| Sunflower Seeds | 24.0 | 375 |
| Salad Oil | 0 | 900 |
| Tomato/Red Pepper | 1.0 | 20 |

## TABLE III.

| | PORTION | WEIGHT IN GRAMS | PROTEIN | CALORIES |
|---|---|---|---|---|
| Avocado | 1 qtr. | 50 | 1.0 | 122.0 |
| Cucumber | 7 slices | 50 | 0.3 | 6.0 |
| Mung Sprouts | 1 cup | 140 | 5.6 | 33.6 |
| Summer Squash | ½ cup | 50 | 0.3 | 8.0 |
| Sunflower Seeds | 2 T. | 25 | 6.0 | 94.0 |
| Leafy Greens | ½ cup | 25 | 0.6 | 5.0 |
| Salad Oil | 1/8 cup | 30 | 0 | 270.0 |
| Tomato/Red Pepper | 2 slices | 20 | .2 | 4.0 |
| Dulse or Kelp | Sm. bits | 10 | 0 | 0.0 |
| TOTAL | | 400 or 14 oz. | 14.0 | 542.6 |

Dr. Harvey C. Lisle's Analysis (continued)

The ingredients required in a complete meal are protein, carbohydrates, fat (oil), minerals, vitamins and enzymes in sufficient quantity and quality to furnish adequate energy (or calories) and elements needed for growth (or maintenance).

A meal prepared from raw garden produce, sprouts and seeds will assuredly be rich in vitamins, minerals and enzymes. By adding a little dulse or kelp to the meal, the flavor is enhanced and the minerals are enriched beyond any doubt of adequacy. Such a meal provides a wider range of vitamins, minerals and enzymes, and in larger quantities than in the more conventional salad of lettuce, tomato, cucumber and onion, which is often grown on chemicalized, depleted soils and suffers further nutritional loss during transportation and shelf-life than the freshly gathered sprouts and indoor greens which enter into the "complete meal salad" immediately after harvest. The salad oil, and the avocado, which contains 26.4% fat, assures a rich supply of high quality fat and carbohydrates, which are considered "go" or energy foods.

The "complete meal salad" contains proteins which correspond in quantity and quality much more closely with man's requirements than meat and the typical "mixed" diet which supply excessive amounts of protein.

Years ago, science considered 120 grams of protein to be the daily requirement of the average person; presently this figure has been reduced to 70 grams.

Statements the usual "professional" nutritionist might make concerning the meal are, "Vitamin B-12 is only produced in flesh food," or, "There is no animal protein in the meal."

However, science has discovered that in vegetarian animals Vitamin B-12 is manufactured by bacteria in the intestines.

Dr. Wolfgang Tiling of Hamburg, Germany discovered the synthesis of Vitamin B-12 in the intestines of children who were on a soy milk diet.*

Animal protein has to be broken down into simple amino acids before it can be reconstructed into human protein. In meat eaters, putrefactive bacteria predominate and most of the meat rots in the lengthy human intestines, placing an excessive strain on the liver, which is not equipped for elimination of large quantities of uric acid and other toxic by-products of meat eating, and these toxins are often absorbed into the tissue of the organism.

In plant life, much of the protein is already in a pre-digested state; this is especially true of sprouts and indoor greens, where most of the protein is in the form of simple amino acids. Furthermore, the protein in plants has the advantage of being free from nuculeo proteins and therefore does not lead to the formation of uric acid in the system and does not encourage gout or rheumatism.

New scientific findings indicate the amount of protein required of raw food can vary from 20-50 grams for each individual, depending on weight, sex, climate and type of work.

Dr. M. Hindhede, Director of the Hindhede Laboratory for Nutritional Research established by the Danish government, shows the definite relationship between high protein diets, acidosis and disease. It is a scientifically demonstrated fact, for example, that dairy cows, which are fed heavily on proteins, are shorter lived and subject to many disorders of the kidneys and bowels not found in cows which are permitted to graze and eat in a more normal manner.

The work of Dr. Joseph Good has dramatically pointed out that low protein diet in animals and humans yields an increased resistance to disease, and builds an immunity against cancer. He found it nearly impossible to graft cancer cells on species fed on a low protein diet.

(*Soybeans, P. Chen, Ph.D., Chemical Elements Pub., Mass.)

Protein is constructed of 22 building blocks called amino acids, of which 8 have been found essential in the food requirements of man. From these 8, he can synthesize the others he requires. All 8 of these essential amino acids must be present together in the "complete meal" as they complement each other's qualities. If one of the 8 is missing, then the remaining amino acids cannot be utilized and fail to provide as they were designed to.

The following is a description of these eight essential amino acids:

**LEUCINE** and **ISOLEUCINE** have a decisive influence upon the function of digestive enzymes in the stomach, pancreas and small intestines.

**LYSINE** is critically necessary, for if lysine is low, the assimilation of all other amino acids is impaired. Lack of it may lead to slow growth, anemia, reproductive problems, pneumonia, and acidosis. We require larger amounts of lysine than the other amino acids.

**METHIONINE** deals with fat metabolism. Liver degeneration and rheumatic fever are dangers of too little methionine. Rats go on a hunger strike, sicken and die in about six weeks if not fed methionine.

**PHENYLALANINE** is associated with good utilization of vitamin C and in necessary for the production of thyroxin, the iodine containing hormone.

**TRYPTOPHANE** is associated with a healthy skin, healthy hair and good utilization of the B vitamins, pyridoxine and niacin.

**THREONINE** makes the build-up of the body tissues efficient and thereby supports the utilization of nutrients in food.

**VALINE** is extremely important to the nervous system.

Assuming the same amount of protein will be ingested per meal for the other two meals of the day, the total protein intake will come to 45 grams.

Again assuming that the person who partakes of the "complete meal salad" is on somewhat of a natural food regimen, he will instinctively know whether the meal is satisfying or is too much or not enough. With good judgement, the individual may take the "complete meal salad" and adjust it to his or her own personal requirements. It will maintain good health in body, mind, and spirit.

## *SOME LETTERS FROM LIVE FOODS FANS*

I recently heard of your book "How I Conquered Cancer Naturally" and your appearance on the 700 Club. Four years ago my husband was being crippled by arthritis and through prayer and a good deal of searching we found a doctor who guided us in nutrition and my husband now does not take any medication at all and he feels and looks better than he did ten years ago.

When the doctor who had been treating him medically saw the improvement in him he dismissed it as a temporary remission... On Sunday while leaving church, an older women told me her husband had gone through the same pattern...terribly ill then healing through nutrition and spiritual faith, and that his so called "temporary remission" has now lasted twenty-two years. We are very grateful to the Lord that my husband's temporary remission is now over forty months long.

M.M.Z., Stratford, CT

**CHAPTER XI.**

 **ALL DAY LOAF**

**2 c. sunflower seeds**

Soak sunflower seeds overnite. Grind in grinder and blend with Rejuvelac to a thick paste. Let stand at room temperature all day. Add to:

| | |
|---|---|
| **1 red pepper, chopped fine** | **2-3 tomatoes, chopped fine** |
| **¼ c. parsley, chopped fine** | **Basil** |
| **1 clove garlic, pressed** | **Caraway seed** |
| **1 c. mushrooms, chopped fine** | **Dill seed** |
| **2 carrots, grated** | |

Mix all ingredients together. Season with basil, caraway seed, and dill seed. Form a loaf. Top with a tomato sauce or seed sauce. As an added attraction, you could grind up some pumpkin seeds (pepitas) and add to the loaf, but they are not a needed ingredient.

 **AVOCADO BRAVO**

| | |
|---|---|
| **2 avocados** | **Spanish sauce** |
| **Pinto beans (that have been** | **Cheddar cheese** |
| **slowly cooked over low heat)** | **Ortega chili pepper (chopped)** |

Halve the avocados, fill with pinto beans. Top with spanish sauce, melted cheese and ortega pepper.

 **CARROT SEED LOAF**

Soak overnight, then grind in grinder:

| | |
|---|---|
| **1 part sunflower seeds** | **1 part chick peas (garbanzo** |
| **1 part sesame seeds** | **beans** |

Combine with:

| | |
|---|---|
| **1 part finely grated carrots** | **Bell pepper finely chopped** |
| **Tomatoes, finely chopped** | **Parsley, finely chopped** |

Season with:

| | |
|---|---|
| **Caraway seed** | **Rejuvelac** |
| **Basil** | |

Moisten with Rejuvelac and form into a loaf.

 **CELERYBURGER**

| | |
|---|---|
| 6 stalks of celery | 1 avocado |
| 1 c. pecans | 6 sprigs parsley |
| 2 T. ripe olives, chopped | ½ tsp. sage |
| 2 green onions | Radishes |

Grind 6 stalks of celery, the onions, and parsley through food grinder. Drain juice for drinking. Grind pecans fine. Mash avocado. Combine all but radishes. Shape into patties. Serve on lettuce leaf. Garnish with radishes. Top with Simple sauce.

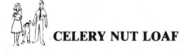 **CELERY NUT LOAF**

| | |
|---|---|
| 2 c. ground or grated celery drained | 3 T. minced parsley |
| | Juice of a small lemon |
| 1 c. ground almonds | ½ tsp. sage or thyme |
| 1 mashed avocado | 2 T. mayonnaise or seed |
| 3 T. minced onion | sauce |

Mix altogether and pack into a loaf pan. Chill. Suggest you top each portion of the loaf with Tomato Lemon Sauce, or if you prefer a hot sauce, Salsa.

 **CHRISETTES**

| | |
|---|---|
| 2 c. fresh peas (or 1 pkg frozen peas) | ½ c. sunflower seeds |
| | 2 tsp. kelp |
| 2 c. diced, raw carrots | Pinch of oregano |
| 2 green onions | |

Grind peas, carrots, onion and sunflower seeds. Mix together and add kelp and oregano. Form into patties. Top with mayonnaise or seed sauce.

**FARMER'S CHOP SUEY**

from Raychel Solomon, Hippocrates Health Institute, Lemon Grove, CA.

| | |
|---|---|
| **1 bunch radishes** | **1 bunch scallions** |
| **½ c. seed sauce** | **3 tomatoes** |
| **1 c. almonds** | **3 T. Dr. Bronner's liquid** |
| **3 T. dill weed** | **bouillon** |
| **4 cucumbers** | **1 tsp. cumin** |

Mix cubed cucumbers, chunks of radishes, sliced green onions, diced tomatoes. Add cumin, dill weed. Add Dr. Bronner's liquid to ground almonds. Put vegetables in refrigerator till ready, then combine with sauce.

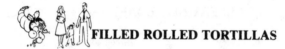**FILLED ROLLED TORTILLAS**

**Corn tortillas**                              **\*Guacamole**

Warm the tortillas in oven. Spread guacamole on ⅓ of the tortilla, including one edge. Roll so guacamole is in the center.

Place two on each plate and dress with \*Mexican sauce.

\*See recipes pages 95, 96 & Page 103.

 **GERMAN TOSTADA**

| | |
|---|---|
| **Corn tortillas (flat)** | **Onions (chopped)** |
| **Sauerkraut (preferably** | **Bell peppers (chopped)** |
| **homemade sauerkraut)** | **Corn(in summer, cut from** |
| | **fresh cobs)** |

Top a corn tortilla with sauerkraut. Top sauerkraut with chopped bell peppers and chopped onions. In summer top all with corn.

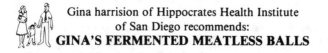

Gina harrision of Hippocrates Health Institute
of San Diego recommends:

## GINA'S FERMENTED MEATLESS BALLS

¾ c. ground sesame seeds
¼ c. ground sunflower seeds
Rejuvelac
Chopped parsley
Green onions, chopped fine
Bell peppers, chopped fine

Celery, chopped fine
Dr. Bronner's seasoning
or tamari
Sweet basil
Celery seed

Moisten the ground seeds with Rejuvelac. Add all other ingredients. Form into balls and let sit for about 10 hours.

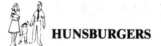

## HUNSBURGERS

1 c. almonds
1 c. pecans
¼ c. pignolias
2 stalks celery
1 large carrot
Few leaves celantro
chopped ripe olives (optional)

1 sm. bell pepper or 1 fresh
pimiento pepper
3 T. onion
1 T. kelp
1 T. vegetable seasoning

Grind through a food grinder and form into a loaf or patties. Garnish with tomatoes and parsley.

## HUNZA PIZZA

Use Hunza bread recipes and roll very thin to fit round pizza pan. Bake in 350 degree oven for 20 minutes. Spread with red salsa taco sauce. Sprinkle with chopped bell peppers, chopped tomatoes, chopped hot peppers, chopped celery, onions, squash, avocado, garlic and . . . or . . . broccoli, mushrooms, or egg plant. (all raw)

 **MEAT LOAF #1**

1 part sunflower and sesame meal
1 part chick peas or
  lentils, sprouted
1 part grated fine carrot
Rejuvelac

Tomatoes, cut up to taste
Pepper, finely cut to taste
Parsley, chopped fine
Caraway seed to taste
Basil to taste

  Mix together the first two ingredients with enough Rejuvelac to make a paste (thick) in the morning. Let stand at room temperature all day. At dinner time mix all the ingredients and form into a loaf.
  Serve with hot sauce.

 **MEAT LOAF #2**

1 part sunflower seed meal
1 part finely grated carrot
Red pepper, finely chopped
Parsley, finely chopped
Garlic, put through a press
Rejuvelac

Mushrooms, chopped
Tomatoes, chopped fine
Basil to taste
Caraway seed to taste
 2 tomatoes, blended

  Start with the sunflower seed meal in the morning, use Rejuvelac to make a thick paste, let stand at room temperature all day. Ground pumpkin seed meal can be used in place of the sunflower seed meal. At dinner time mix all the ingredients and form into a loaf, serve with a sauce made by blending tomatoes.

 **MEXICAN SUCCOTASH**

1 lb. zucchini, chopped
1 onion, chopped
1 clove garlic, minced
1 sm. tomato, peeled
  and chopped

½ tsp. kelp
1 c. fresh corn cut off the cob
1-2 peeled green chilies,
  diced fine
2 T. oil

  Mix all together well. Let stand half hour.

**MOCK TUNA**

| | |
|---|---|
| 1 c. alfalfa sprouts | 1 T. fermented sesame sauce |
| ¼ c. mung sprouts | 1 T. onion |
| ¼ c. lentil sprouts | 1 T. parsley |
| ½ c. celery | 3 T. almond butter |
| 1 T. kelp or more | |

Combine celery, seed sauce, almond butter in blender with a little water. Blend until smooth. Add mung and lentil sprouts in blender. Blend sauce mixture and sprouts just until sprouts are chopped. Stir sprout and sauce mixture into alfalfa sprouts with a spoon (in a bowl). Fill tomato cups and serve on a bed of lettuce.

Sat Kartar and Sat Tirath recommend their Mock Tuna recipe from the Hippocrates Health Institute of San Diego

 **MOCK TUNA**

| | |
|---|---|
| 1½ c. almonds, ground | 2 stalks celery, chopped fine |
| 4 organic carrots, juiced | Dr. Bronner's Mineral |
| 3 oz. Rejuvelac | Bouillon to taste |
| 1 bunch green onions, | Dill weed to taste |
| chopped fine | Cumin powder to taste |
| 2 green peppers, ground fine | Sweet basil to taste |

Mix carrot pulp and ground almonds together. You should have almost equal parts of almond and carrot pulp. Add Rejuvelac. Begin to add carrot juice until desired consistency is attained. You will probably have some juice left over. Mix in rest of ingredients, flavoring to taste. Press into a square pen. Cut into squares.

Mock Tuna is now ready to eat, or may be incubated for fermentation (approx. 6 hrs). If you are not going to incubate, the Rejuvelac can be omitted.

**MOCK TUNA VEGETABLE LOAF**
from Raychel Solomon, Hippocrates Health Institute

| | |
|---|---|
| ⅓ c. almonds | 1 c. sesame seeds |
| 1 c. carrot pulp | ½ bunch finely chopped parsley |
| 2 stalks celery | 1 green pepper |
| 1 c. chopped green onions | Dill weed |
| Basil | Dr. Bronner's liquid |
| 1/8 c. Rejuvelac | bouillon to taste |

Grind almonds and sesame seeds and put in mixing bowl. Add carrot pulp, parsley, finely chopped vegetables, and remaining ingredients. Mix well with hands. If mixture is too thick (for forming into loaf) add Rejuvelac a little bit at a time. Place into baking dish or pan. Incubate 6 to 8 hours.

 **NUT CHEESE**

| | |
|---|---|
| 1 c. raw unsalted nuts | 1 c. water |

Just cover the nuts with water and soak overnight. Place 1 cup water in the blender and drop in the nuts and blend well until creamy. Leave at room temperature 24 hours. It is excellent for salads or over plain sprouts, but it is very rich, so use sparingly. Refrigerate to keep. (This is a fermented food rich in enzymes.)

 **NUT CHEESE**
from Raychel Solomon, Hippocrates Health Institute, Lemon Grove, CA.

| | |
|---|---|
| 1 c. almonds | 1 c. sesame seeds |
| Rejuvelac | 1 chopped onion |
| 4 cloves garlic | ½ stalk celery |
| 1 T. paprika | 1 T. oregano |
| Dr. Bronner's to taste | |

Grind the almonds and sesame seeds and combine, add Rejuvelac and let sit out overnite. Add chopped onion, garlic, celery, paprika, oregano, and Dr. Bronner's. Spread on zucchini, celery, fennel, etc.

## NUT LOAF
(Filling for sandwich or side dish)

| | |
|---|---|
| 1 c. carrots | 1 c. tomatoes |
| ½ c. chopped parsley | ½ c. bell pepper pieces |
| 1 clove garlic | 2 T. oil |
| Ground nuts | Your favorite herb (mine is sage or dill) |

Put all through a food grinder, mix and pack into a loaf pan to serve or make sandwich.

## POTATO PATTIES

| | |
|---|---|
| 2 finely grated raw potatoes | ¼ c. chopped parsley |
| 1 sm. carrot, grated | 4 green onions, chopped fine |
| ¼ c. ground almond or pecan nuts | Kelp |
| ¼ c. ground sunflower seeds | Vegetable seasoning |

Combine all ingredients and make into patties. Add water to moisten or ly if needed.

## SAUERKRAUT (HOMEMADE) #1

| | |
|---|---|
| Crock (Mine measures 10 inches high, inside diameter 8½ inches) | Dulse leaves - 1 oz. |
| | Red cabbage (I use 4 heads to fill my crock ⅔ full. Dulse discolors white cabbage so I use red) |

One head of red cabbage plus ¼ oz. dulse makes approximately 1 qt. of sauerkraut.

Finely shred 1 head of cabbage. Place in crock and pound with a baseball bat or heavy dowel until juice forms. Add 1 T. of kelp and stir. Place about 10 pieces of dulse (the size of a silver dollar) on top. Repeat until crock is full.

Cover top with cabbage leaves. Place plate on top. Weight down with heavy rock or gallon jug of water, etc. Leave at room temperature for 7-10 days.

## SAUERKRAUT
### (A Fermented Food Rich in Enzymes)

**Cabbage, red, green or both**          **Thyme, dill, kelp**

For variety, juniper berries, carrots, peppers, onions, beets can be added.

Cut vegetables in strips or grate. Layer cabbage in the bottom of a large earthenware pot or krock about 6 inches deep, then sprinkle a handful of juniper berries, then a layer of carrots, a layer of peppers, beets, and onions, then a layer of cabbage, etc. Just cabbage can be done alone if you prefer.

Each layer should be pressed down so that the cabbage will be saturated in its own juice. Repeat the procedure. When the container is full, cover with a clean cloth and a heavy stone cover . . . or a cloth, plate and weight.

About once a week, remove the cloth and wash it and replace it. Keep the pot in the kitchen standing at room temperature for about three weeks (or in a cellar or other storage place). Then remove the foam or mildew from the top; the sauerkraut is ready to eat and store it in glass jars in the refrigerator. Start your next sauerkraut again in the empty pot. You will improve the making of it if you keep it up.

Some people like one week old sauerkraut, taste for yourself.

## SEED BALLS
from Raychel Solomon, Hippocrates Health Institute, Lemon Grove, CA.

**Ground almonds**          **Dr. Bronner's liquid bouillon**
**Ground sunflower seeds**          **to taste**
**Ground sesame seeds**          **Green onions**
**Green peppers**          **Oregano**
**Basil**          **Savory**
**Celery**          **Rejuvelac**

Mix equal parts of ground almonds, sunflower seeds, and sesame seeds. Add Rejuvelac to thick, chewy texture (remember: this mixture must be formed into balls). Mince all vegetables very, very finely. Proportions should be 2 parts vegetables to one part seeds. Add minced vegetables to seed mixture along with Dr. Bronner's bouillon. Mix in spices and blend very well. Put in incubator for 8 to 10 hours.

 **SEED LOAF**

2 c. sesame meal (ground
    sesame seeds
4 c. sunflower meal (ground
    sunflower seeds)
8-10 lg. mushrooms, chopped
Parsley, lots, diced

3 cloves garlic, finely diced
3-6 stalks of celery, finely diced
2 med. onions, diced
Basil, a pinch
Caraway, ground to taste
Vegetable seasoning

Put ground seeds into bowl. Add enough Rejuvelac or water so that the meal sticks together. Add diced vegetables and seasonings according to taste. Form mixture into either balls or loaves. Bake in either sun or warm place (70 degrees - 90 degress) until top is somewhat dried out and it is firm. The longer these sit, the more the flavors will go throughout the loaf. Takes about 12 to 24 hours.

 **MUNG "SPAGETTI"**

Long sprouted mung beans to use as spagetti.
**SESAME BALLS:**
1 c. ground sesame seed (or sun-
    flower seed or mix)
1 clove garlic put through press
2 green onions, chopped

1 tsp. chopped parsley
1/8 tsp. chili powder
½ tsp. kelp
½ tsp. vegetable seasoning

Form into balls.

**SAUCE:**
3 lg. tomatoes
1/8 c. cilantro
½ tsp. oregano
1 tsp. kelp
½ c. celery
¼ c. parsley

½ bell pepper
3 green onions
1 clove garlic put
    through press
1 tsp. vegetable seasoning

Blend in blender or grind in a food grinder. Put sauce over mung sprouts and top with the sesame balls. Or use Gina's fermented meatless balls.

## SURPRISE LOAF

3 c. sesame seeds
3 c. sunflower seeds
1 c. cashew nuts
1 small onion, chopped
2 stalks celery, chopped
Lots of kelp

½ bell pepper, chopped
Some chopped mushrooms
Handful parsley, chopped fine
Pinch of thyme, oregano,
   basil, ground caraway

Grind the seeds and nuts. Mix above ingredients with Rejuvelac to a sticky consistency. Shape into loaves or balls. Place in incubator or other warm place (the sun) to let flavors combine.

## SWEET AND SOUR EGGPLANT

1 med. eggplant, cubed
  (or use zucchini)
Olive or other oil
3 T. kelp
¼ c. apple cider vinegar

1 T. honey
1 tsp. chopped fresh mint
1 tsp. oregano
1 clove garlic, minced

Combine your oil, vinegar, kelp, honey, mint, oregano, and garlic. Mix well. Add cubed eggplant (or zucchini). Allow to marinate for 30 minutes.

## RAW TOSTADA
from Jane of Hippocrates Health Institute

Tortillas
Guacamole (mashed avocado,
  chopped tomatoes, onions,
  lemon juice)
Mung bean sprouts

Lettuce
Tomatoes
Cucumber
Radishes
Sesame seeds

Spread tortillas with guacamole, sprinkle with mung bean sprouts. Toss chopped lettuce, tomatoes, cucumber lightly with oil and vinegar dressing. Top your tortillas with the tossed salad. Sprinkle with sesame seeds. Garnish with radishes and cucumbers.

# JANE MURPHY'S "KISMET" VEGETABLE LOAF
(sun-kissed)

½ c. rolled oats
1 c. Rejuvelac
1 heaping tsp. rice miso (a
 fermented rice paste - buy
 in Health Food Store)
1 tsp. Dr. Bronner's Instant Soup
1 tsp. kelp
¼ tsp. oregano
½ tsp. cumin
2 stalks celery, chopped fine

½ tsp. celery seed
1 tsp. Dr. Bronner's "All
 in One" bouillon
¼ c. cashew nut cheese (the
 starter)
1 c. sunflower seeds, ground fine
4 lg. carrots, ground & juiced
1 med. red onion, chopped fine
1 med. green pepper, chopped
 fine

I.    Prepare ahead: Rejuvelac, Cashew nut cheese.
II.   1. Soak ½ cup rolled oats about 5 hrs. (place in a bowl and
         just cover with water)
      2. Wash and cut into small pieces about 4 large carrots. Grind
         through juicer - using juice and pulp.
      3. Wash and cut into very small pieces green pepper, celery
         and onion.
      4. Put seasonings and Rejuvelac and cheese into blender and
         mix.
III.  1. Grind 1 cup sunflower seeds - put into large bowl. Add oats.
      2. Add liquid from the blender and chopped vegetables and
         ground carrots (with juice).
      3. Mix all ingredients until well blended.
      4. Press into a loaf pan (about 9 x 10 x 2 baking dish) that has
         been lightly oiled. Set in sunlight for rest of day. Put in
         incubator all night and part of the next morning.
IV    1. Incubation: (a) Use a paper sack as an oven. Place pan
         inside sack with open end butted up to refrigerator heat
         outlet. This is a warm, constant gentle heat that will allow
         food to ferment at room temperature. (b) Cover pan and
         put it in your bed under the electric blanket turned on low*
         as an alternative. (Excellent yogurt can be made by this in-
         cubation method!)
      2. Other bases instead of oatmeal (raw): corn meal, millet
         (cooked), sunflower seeds or sesame seeds.

*  Should be around 80 to 90 degrees.

 **VEGETABLE LOAF**

from Raychel Solomon, Director of Hippocrated Health Institute
of San Diego

| | |
|---|---|
| **8 carrots** | **½ bunch celery** |
| **1 green pepper** | **1 bunch green onions** |
| **1 c. ground sunflower seeds** | **½ c. whole sunflower seeds** |
| **½ c. fermented seed sauce** | **Vegetable seasoning to taste** |
| **Caraway seeds, ground** | **1 T. oregano** |
| **1 T. cumin** | |

Juice carrots. Serve juice. Take pulp and put in large bowl. Mince finely the celery, green peppers and green onions. Add to carrot pulp. Mix in remaining ingredients and thoroughly, by hand, blend all ingredients well. Put in incubator or in sun, uncovered, for 6 to 8 hours (incubator makes a crust). Serve as main course.

Note: Put mixture in a baking dish or baking pan and then incubate.

**CHAPTER XII.**

## AVOCADO SUNFLOWER SMOOTHIE
(Sandwich filling) from Mrs. Fred H. Langford

1 c. sunflower seeds covered with
water & soaked overnight
2 avocados
½ c. sliced carrots - thin sliced

1 clove garlic
½ c. chopped parsley
1 tsp. caraway seed

Place avocados and other ingredients in blender. Add seeds slowly and blend until smooth. The sunflower seeds may be replaced by cashews.

## EYDIE MAE'S CALIFORNIA SANDWICH

Corn tortillas
Avocado, sliced or mashed
Kelp and veg. seasoning
Lemon juice

Raw mushrooms
Hot chili peppers, chopped fine
Sweet bell peppers, chopped fine
Sunflower seeds
Alfalfa sprouts

Mash your avocado or slice and season with kelp and vegetable seasoning, and lemon juice. Warm your tortillas. Spread with mashed avocado or sliced avocado, add hot chili peppers or sweet bell peppers depending upon your taste, or both. Add raw mushroom slices and sprinkle with sunflower seeds. Top with alfalfa sprouts (a good covering). I serve them open face at home, but put a second tortilla on top for a box lunch (or a brown bag). Delicious! Radishes also make a good addition.

## FALAFEL

4 c. sprouted chick-peas
(garbanzo beans)
1 T. kelp

¼ tsp. mixed ground herbs,
basil, majoram, thyme
½ tsp. hot chili

Grind beans and chili in fine blade of food chopper. Mix in kelp and herbs. Use as a side dish, a sandwich filling or thin with Rejuvelac or water and make a sauce.

 **GARDEN TACOS**

Corn tortillas
Anaheim peppers (mildly hot)
  chopped fine
Floral gem peppers (hot),
  chopped fine
Pinto bean sprouts, mashed
Sunflower seeds
Raw mushrooms, sliced

Avocados, sliced
Alfalfa sprouts or other
  favorite sprouts
Cherry tomatoes, halved, or
  sliced tomatoes
Red salsa sauce
Green tomatillo sauce

Combinations are endless. Start with corn tortillas (first wrapped in foil and heated in your oven) sliced with avocados, or pinto bean sprouts mashed, and built from there with your favorite sprouts, topping with either red salsa sauce, or the green tomatillo sauce, sunflower seeds, tomatoes, and chopped peppers. Make your own Dagwood.

 **MUSHROOM SANDWICH FILLING**

1 c. coarsely chopped mushrooms
  (fresh)
2 green onions, chopped

Kelp to taste
Mayonnaise to moisten enough
  to spread

**NUT BUTTER**

Unsalted, uncooked nuts

Put through a juicer such as the Champion or a Norwalk. This will grind them up like peanut butter. If dry, a small amount of oil may be added while grinding.

 **ONION SANDWICH**

Tortillas or Wayfarer bread
Thinly sliced Bermuda onions
  (or your favorite)

Thinly sliced cucumber or
  alfalfa sprouts
Mayonnaise or seed sauce

Spread bread well with mayonnaise. Layer with onions and sprouts or onions and cucumbers.

 **CALIFORNIA TOSTADA**

Corn tortillas (without
  preservatives)
Warm cooked pinto beans
Tossed green salad

Avocado dip
Alfalfa sprouts or mung
  bean sprouts
Radlishes, parsley, and
  cherry tomatoes

Blend pinto beans in a little hot water (or mash). Spread on tortilla (heated). Add a layer of tossed salad. Top this with avocado dip. Top this with sprouts. Garnish with radishes, parsley and cherry tomatoes. Serve open face with garnishes on the side.

CHAPTER XIII.

## COCONUT CEREAL

1 coconut                              Milk from 1 coconut

Remove the milk and the meat from the coconut. Blend all in blender. Spoon into cereal bowl. Dates or honey may be added depending upon taste.

## FRUIT CEREAL

½ c. raisins                          2 figs
6 dates

Soak the above ingredients overnight.

1 c. of wheat from Rejuvelac         ¼ c. sesame seeds
1 apple                              1 c. oat flakes, granola or
½ c. sunflower seeds                     other cereal

Blend in blender soaked wheat from Rejuvelac, apple, seeds, Rejuvelac to puree consistency. Add raisins, figs, dates, quickly blend. Remove from blender. Stir in cereal.

## NYVA STEWART'S GRANOLA

Mix:
4 c. rolled oats                     ½ c. sesame seeds
1½ c. shredded unsweetened           ½ c. flax seeds
    coconut                          ½ c. bran
1 c. wheat germ                      ½ c. ground roasted soybeans
1 c. chopped nuts
1 c. hulled sunflower seeds

Heat:
½ c. oil (soy, sesame or corn)       ½ tsp. vanilla
½ c. honey

Add the above to dry ingredients and mix (will be dry). Spread mixture on cookie sheet with sides and bake at 325 degrees about 15 minutes.

 **WHEAT GUM, CEREAL & MILK**

Take one day wheat sprouts, (a handful) and chew until it is the consistency of gum . . . a delightful, healthy gum. Or you can use wheat left over from making Rejuvelac.

—The soaked wheat that is used to make Rejuvelac, kept without water for 15 hours will sprout slightly and may be used to make a breakfast cereal, a milk, gum, or plant to produce wheat grass.

—To make the delicious cereal, blend one cup of the slightly sprouted wheat seeds and ½ to 1 cup of water until the consistency you enjoy.

—To make the tasty milk, blend together one cup of the slightly sprouted wheat and two cups of warm water and strain.

## SOME LETTERS FROM LIVE FOODS FANS

I am as convinced as Eydie of the importance of her diet. My mother died of cancer; my father from a heart attack. I began reading books on health and nutrition. I became a vegetarian and started a ritual of periodic fasting and colonics. I never felt better in my life. My acne cleared up as well as constipation problems, stuffy nose and lower back aches.

M. A. S., Portland, OR

**CHAPTER XIV.**

 ## UNCOOKED APPLE SAUCE

**3 organic sweet apples**          **½ c. water**

Cut up the apples, peels, cores, seeds and all. Pour ½ cup water into blender. Drop in the cut up apples. Do not blend too long, or they will oxidize. Eat right away. If your apples are not organically grown, remove the pits and do not use.

 ## APRICOT DELIGHT

**6 apricots, pitted & sliced**          **Huckleberries**
**2 sweet apples, cut up**                **1 pear, diced**
                                          **2 green plates**

Mix together sliced apricots, cut-up apples, and huckleberries. Arrange them on green plates (if you have them), Sprinkle with diced pear.

 ## BONANZA SPLIT

**2 bananas, sliced in half**          **2 bunches seedless grapes**
**   lengthwise**
**1 papaya, cut-up in pieces**         **1 persimmon, diced fine**
**1 mango, cut-up**                    **2 banana split dishes**

Place the bananas lengthwise in the bottom of the banana split dishes. Put a pile of grapes in the center on top of the banana. Pile up papaya pieces on one end and mango pieces on the other end on top of the banana. Sprinkle persimmon on top.

## CANDY KISSES

from Ann Wigmore -
Hippocrates Health Institute of Boston

**#1 - 1 fresh coconut**
**2 c. almonds, ground, or 1 c.**
**sesame seeds, ground & 2 T. honey**

Grate fresh coconut. Add almonds or sesame, honey mixture. Form into balls and roll in dried coconut.

**#2 - ½ lb. dates (or figs or raisins    Coconut**
**Sesame seeds, ground**

Run fruit through a meat grinder. Add equal amonts of sesame seeds and coconut and run through fooder grinder again. Roll in coconut. Wrap in wax paper and refrigerate.

## CARROT CAKE

**1 lb. fresh pitted dates        2 fresh coconuts**
**1 lb. carrot pulp (from juicing-    4 T. honey**
**2 lbs. carrots make about 1 lb. pulp)**

Juice your carrots. Use the juice for drinking. Finely grate the white meat of the coconut. Use the liquid inside your coconut for drinking. Put dates and carrot pulp through a food chopper (meat grinder) to mix well. Add ½ the grated coconut; blend by hand in a large bowl, then run through the food chopper again. Press ½ of mixture into an 8" square pan. To ½ of the remaining coconut add 2 T. honey and blend by hand. Spread evenly over first layer. Add 2nd half of mixture and press firmly in pan. Put aside about 3 T. of plain coconut for topping. Combine the rest with the remaining 2 T. of honey and spread evenly over top. Sprinkle on the 3 T. of plain coconut and press firmly. This may be garnished with nut halves or pieces if desired. Cover with wax paper and put in refrigerator to harden.

## COCONUT DATE LOGS

| | |
|---|---|
| 1-8 oz. pkg. pitted dates, chopped | ¾ c. finely chopped nuts |
| ½ c. butter | ¾ c. granola |
| 1 tsp. vanilla | ¾ c. unsweetened coconut |

In a pan, combine dates, butter and vanilla. Place over low heat and stir until butter melts and blends with dates. Chill until firm enough to hold its shape. Add nuts and granola and mix thoroughly. Sprinkle the coconut on a plate. Take 1 T. of mixture and roll into a log about 1½" long. Then roll in coconut to cover. Chill.

## COCONUT FRUIT PIE
from Ann Wigmore -
Hippocrates Health Institute of Boston

**PIE CRUSTS** (use either):
#1  Shredded coconuts (freshly made).
#2  Shredded coconuts combined with mashed soft dates or date paste.
#3  Place a coconut through a juicer and use only the pulp. This extracts the fat content from the coconut.
Add almond butter to help shape into pie pan. (May also add carob powder for color or flavor if desired.)

**FILLINGS** (Use either)
#1  Combine grated peeled apples and cinnamon. Sprinkle top with coconut and/or raisins for decorations.
#2  Use any fresh cut-up fruits. To insure firmer consistency place in freezer for a few hours.

## DATE PECAN ROLLS

| | |
|---|---|
| 2 c. dates | Dried coconut |
| ½ c. pecans | |

Put dates and pecans through the meat grinder. Form into rolls or balls and roll in coconut.

## DRIED FRUIT CANDIES — APRICOT
### from Ann Wigmore -
### Hippocrates Heath Institute of Boston

| | |
|---|---|
| **1 c. moist packed apricots** | **1 T. orange juice** |
| **(or soak to moisten)** | **4 T. finely chopped almonds** |
| **⅓ c. fresh grated or dried coconut** | |

Put apricots through a food chopper. Mix in the coconut and orange juice and grind again. Divide into 4 equal parts, wrap in saran wrap, foil or waxed paper and chill thoroughly. Use one part at a time and roll on a board with your hands to form a long roll (14-16 inches long) sprinkling the board with about 1 T. finely chopped almonds. Slice in 2" pieces.

## PEAR

| | |
|---|---|
| **6 oz. pears (dried)** | **1 T. lemon juice** |
| **4 T. unsweetened coconut** | |

Prepare in the same way as the dried apricots, only roll in coconut instead of nuts.

## PRUNE

| | |
|---|---|
| **6 oz. prunes** | **½ tsp. grated lemon peel** |
| **½ c. chopped walnuts** | **1 T. lemon juice** |
| **1 T. coconut** | **1 T. finely chopped walnuts** |

Prepare in the same way as the apricots, only combine prunes, coconut, lemon peel and juice, and roll in 1 T. finely chopped walnuts.

## DRIED FRUIT COOKIES

| | |
|---|---|
| 1 c. prunes | 1 c. dried pears |
| 1 c. apricots | |

Soak the above ingredients for several hours and drain.

| | |
|---|---|
| 1 c. raisins | 1 orange |
| 1 c. dates | 1 lemon |
| 1 c. figs | |

Grate the rind of the orange and the lemon. Put all fruits through a meat grinder. Add orange and lemon rind. This should be a sticky consistency.

**Optional: Ground sunflower seeds      Lemon juice**
**          if more body is needed   Carob**
**              Vanilla**

Add lemon juice or sunflower seeds as needed. Form into rolls, wrap in wax paper and chill. Slice to serve.
Variations: Roll in grated coconut or ground nuts.
      2.  or Use sesame seed instead of sunflower seeds.
      3.  or Add mashed bananas.

## FRESH FRUIT WHIP

**Any favorite fruit                1 c. fruit juice**

Add enough fresh fruit in your blender to 1 cup of the same fruit juice to make a soft whip consistency.
A pleasing drink is:

**#1.  Apple juice**
     **Apples and/or pears**
**#2.  Peach juice**
     **Peaches or/and apricots**
**#3.  Pineapple juice**
     **Pineapple**
**#4.  Berries alone may be run in the blender to make a whip.**

 **FROZEN ICES**

| | |
|---|---|
| Frozen peeled bananas | Frozen fresh peaches |
| Frozen peeled oranges | Frozen fresh apricots |
| Frozen berries | |

Put one of your choice through the food grinder (or juicer if you have a Champion or Norwalk). Serve in a sherbert dish.

 **FRUIT DELIGHT**

| | |
|---|---|
| Raisins | Apples |
| Dates | Sunflower seeds |
| Figs | Sesame seeds |
| Soaked wheat from 3 day | Rejuvelac |
|    Rejuvelac | |

Soak first three ingredients overnight. Blend all ingredients together, adding enough Rejuvelac to make a puree. Makes a delightful breakfast or supper.

 **FRUIT NUT LOG**

| | |
|---|---|
| 1 c. dried figs | 1 tsp. grated lemon peel |
| 1 c. pitted dates | 4 T. lemon juice |
| 1 c. raisins | 1 c. almond butter |
| 1 c. unsweetened coconut | ½ c. ground nuts |
| 1 c. chopped nuts | |

Put the first five ingredients through the food grinder twice. Add lemon juice and peel and blend well with a spoon. Divide mixture into 2 equal parts and shape each part into a roll about 12 inches long. Roll each log in ¼ cup ground nuts. Wrap tightly and chill. Slice and serve.

You may omit nuts and substitute 1 cup granola in the original grinding. Then roll your log in ⅓ cup of crushed cereal.

## FUDGE
from Marilyn Spillman

| | |
|---|---|
| 1 c. almond butter | 1 tsp. vanilla |
| 1 c. honey | 2 c. grated coconut |
| 1 c. carob powder | |

Mix all ingredients together and cut in squares or roll into balls.

## ICE CREAM

| | |
|---|---|
| 2 c. soy milk powder | ⅓ c. nuts |
| 2 c. fruit or 1 c. carob | 1 tsp. lethecin |
| | ½ tsp. kelp |

MIx all together in your blender. Freeze.

## MELON BALLS

| | |
|---|---|
| Cantelope | Watermelon |
| Honeydew melons | |

Use melon ball cutter to make a bowl of canteloupe and honeydew melon balls. Watermelon may also be served. Place in a bowl with toothpicks handy for guests or serve in individual pretty glass dishes.

## PEAR PERFECTION

| | |
|---|---|
| Fresh pears | Diced fruit |
| Orange juice | |

Peel pears; sprinkle with orange juice to prevent darkening. Top halves with diced fruit. Serve with dressing if desired.

## PINEAPPLE BOAT

1 fresh pineapple
2 fresh oranges
Mint for garnish

2 fresh grapefruit
Optional: tangerines, tangelos,
any citrus fruit

Cut pineapple in half lengthwise. Hollow out, leaving on the top leaves. Filled with cubed pineapple, orange, graprfruit, etc.

This may be topped with an orange sherbert made from frozen oranges put through a Champion or Norwalk juicer or a meat grinder.

## PINEAPPLE WHIP DRESSING

1 can frozen pineapple concentrate
1 fresh pineapple, cut up

Bananas

Liquify in blender the first 2 ingredients; then add one banana to each cup of pineapple mixture. Blend well.

Use as a dressing for fruit cups or fruit salads, or serve as a whipped desert. Top with a red grape or a piece of red apple.

## SPROUTED SUNFLOWER COOKIES

2 c. sprouted sunflower seeds
6 soft dates
½ c. raisins

½ c. nut butter
1 T. ground orange peel

Place on a wooden board and chop the first 3 ingredients. Add orange peel & enough nut butter to make mixture hold together. Form into balls and/or other creative shapes, or one large block and refrigerate. When cold, cut into individual squares and wrap in saran wrap.

Variations: Add 2 soft black figs to the above mixture during the first step.

Add 2 T. ground sesame seeds during the first step.

 **STUFFED DATES**

**Pitted dates**            **Coconut**
**Nut butter**              **Half pecans**

Fill the pitted dates with nut butter. Roll in coconut. Place a pecan half on top.

 **TROPICAL DELIGHT**
from Betty Simms - Missionary from the Philippines

**1 mango**                 **1 banana**
**1 papaya**                **A little water**

Peel the fruit. Blend in blender at high speeds until smooth. Serve in clear glasses or your prettiest bowls.

This has become a big favorite of ours, and was given to me by Mrs. Art Simms (Betty), missionary visiting here from the Philippines, when she stayed with me several days. *E.M.*

# WHAT IS WHEATGRASS

**CHAPTER XV.**

# WHAT IS WHEAT GRASS?

Have you ever seen a field of wheat? This is wheat grass.

It is planted from hard red winter wheat seeds (or berries). Wheat seeds are available at most health food stores, or they will usually order them for you.

Use soft, spring wheat for summer planting and making Rejuvelac.

## HOW TO GROW WHEAT GRASS OUTDOORS

1. Punch or drill holes in the bottoms of pans (cookie sheets, roasting pans, etc.).
2. Fill pans with good soil to almost level with pan top for ease of harvesting. No peat moss or ditches around edge needed.
3. Spread top with wheat berries that have been soaked overnight (12 to 15 hours).
4. Turn identical pan upside down over wheat to form lid.
5. Lift lid several times a day to moisten wheat.
6. Remove lid after sprouting.
7. Harvest wheat grass when 7" to 8" tall.

HOW TO GROW WHEAT GRASS INDOORS is found in the book, *How I Conquered Cancer Naturally* by Eydie Mae with Chris Loeffler, $2.95 from Production House, 4307 Euclid Ave., San Diego, CA. 92115, or $3.95 from Harvest House, 17845 Sky Park Circle, Irvine, CA. 92714.

Wheat grass may be cut up fine in salads, but the most benefits are from juicing it as the fiber is hard to digest. See information on juicers on page 159.

## INTERESTING BITS OF KNOWLEDGE

**CASHEW NUTS** - are imported from India. They are poison when picked, and heat or chemically treated to remove the poisonous husks. Then they are fumigated before being brought into the U.S. Eydie Mae does not eat them. Chris eats a few now and then.

**SPRAYED APPLES** - Eydie Mae was told that apples are sprayed with 18 different sprays which penetrate the skin. The seeds will absorb and retain up to 75 percent of the spray. Eydie Mae does not eat them, just organically grown apples, unsprayed. Chris peels them and cores and seeds them when she is unable to get organically grown apples.

**LECINAISE** - In march of 1977, the FDA recalled all Lecinaise (the commerical product) because the manufacturer claims that there are no eggs in it. According to the FDA, Lecinaise contains eggs, salt and a preservative. Suggest you make your own mayonnaise from the recipes in this book.

**SEEDS** - To grind seeds, use a nut or seed grinder or a coffee grinder, available in most Health Food Stores.

## WHERE TO BUY

**JUICERS:**  Most Health Food Stores sell a variety of juicers.

One distributor we know who has a large variety, from hand juicers to electric juicers, and at all prices, is: Dale Gardner, 6880 Tower, San Diego, Ca. (714) 465-5285. You may have a distributor in your area.

The Bosch is a good electric model juicer though rather expensive. Blenders and juice extractors do not do an adequate job on juicing wheatgrass.

An old fashioned food chopper or meat grinder does the job because it has the worm screw in it, however you would need to squeeze the wheatgrass juice through 2 or 3 layers of cheesecloth to separate the juice from the pulp.

If you are so inclined, a 50-60 output RPM motor with gear reducer ¼ horsepower motor may be put on a hand grinder.

**WHEAT BERRIES:**  Wheat seeds (berries) organically grown are available at Health Food Stores, Natural Food Stores, and Seed Stores.

One good source we know who ships is: Homesteader, 1437 Simpson Way, Escondido, CA. 92025, (714) 743-7007.

**WHEATGRASS:**  Many Health Food Stores and Farmers Markets now sell wheatgrass. Also, individuals are growing it to sell. Watch the classified ads.

# MENUS

## THANKSGIVING

Breakfast - Bonanza split
Noon      - Mushroom salad
            Tabouli salad
            Guacamole Tacos
Evening   - Hunsbergers
            Or Persimmon salad

## CHRISTMAS

Breakfast - Frozen Banana Ice garnished with grapes
Noon      - Carrot juice
            Guacamole stuffed celery
            Crab Salad
Evening   - Tostados
            Or Apple - Pear Smoothies

## EASTER

Breakfast - Tropical Delight
Noon      - Gazpacho Soup with rolled tortillas
            Tossed salad with dressing
Evening   - German tostadas
            Or melon plate

"Build yourselves houses and dwell in them;
plant gardens and eat the fruit of them."

(Jeremiah, 29:5)

# INDEX

FERMENTED FOODS PLUS
SAUCES, RELISHES, DRESSINGS
& DIPS

SPROUTING

## *A LETTER FROM EYDIE*

Dear Friends,

It has been three years since our book "How I Conquered Cancer Naturally" was published. It has been five and one half years since I was diagnosed as having malignant breast cancer.

Today, I feel great, lead a very active life, do a lot of traveling and am looking forward to the years ahead. The "Live Food" diet has proven itself to me.

The picture on the back of the book was taken to assure you that I am still very much alive as so many of you have written and asked.

Have fun with some of these new recipes!

God bless you all.

                                        Eydie Mae